SHRUBS

An Adrian Bloom Gardening Guide

JARROLD COLOUR PUBLICATIONS · NORWICH

What are shrubs?

The term 'shrubs' as applied to those plants described in this book are woody ornamentals which are generally hardy in the United Kingdom. Shrubs can be as low growing as 10 cm (4 in) or as high as perhaps 5 or 6 metres – and at that sort of eventual height a shrub may well be classed as a small tree.

There exists in gardens and in cultivation literally thousands of species and varieties of shrubs for all types of conditions, giving a tremendous range of flower, form and foliage. Many are evergreen, retaining their foliage throughout the year, though the majority are deciduous, dropping their leaves in the winter. Though there are many native shrubs, a great proportion of those in our gardens have originated from all parts of the world and have undoubtedly enhanced the selection we have available to beautify our gardens.

Why are they good garden plants?

As with Hardy Perennials there are plants in the shrub range for almost any given position, almost any garden or personal taste.

There are evergreen shrubs such as Laurels which provide a screen or shelter from noise and wind and a backcloth for more showy plants; there are deciduous shrubs which flower in winter such as Chimonanthus, The Winter Sweet. There are those which furnish good autumn leaf colour such as Enkianthus or some of the Berberis family; many which provide beautiful fragrant flowers such as some of the Daphnes or Philadelphus, The Mock Orange and even those like the Hamamelis which offer winter flowers, fragrance *and* autumn colour!

Many shrubs are notable for the colour of their bark in winter, when the bare stems of willows and some of the Cornus stand out in the sun. Climbers will be covered in another publication but there are shrubs such as Pyracanthas which can be adapted perfectly to grow against a wall.

There are shrubs for larger gardens and more and more these days dwarf shrubs for the modern smaller garden. Shrubs associate well with other shrubs and they also fit in happily with other hardy plants such as conifers, perennials and alpines – but as always it is important to select shrubs which fit in well in scale and appearance.

Left: Potentilla fruticosa *'Tilford Cream' makes a good foreground plant. Behind is* Kolkwitzia amabilis *'Pink Cloud'. Right:* Fuchsia, *backed by* Lavandula *'Hidcote Blue' and* Hypericum patulum *'Hidcote'*

Foreground: Juniperus *'Old Gold'. The purple-leaved* Berberis thunbergii *'Red Chief' is next to* Cornus alba *'Spaethii' and* Hosta sieboldiana *'Elegans'. The tree is* Robinia pseudoacacia *'Frisia'*

3

What are their likes and dislikes?

Because of the vast range of shrubs there is, inevitably, a great variance in the type of conditions that they like or dislike. It must certainly be a general rule that if a shrub is recommended for a warm, well-drained sunny position then it will dislike a cold, badly drained north-facing aspect! Not all plants are so simple in their tastes and there are many shrubs that will thrive almost anywhere. Advice is given in the following text on the particular likes or dislikes of individual families (genera) or varieties.

However, it is worth bringing up the question of lime-lovers (preferring alkaline soils) and lime-haters (preferring acid soils) since this is the most fundamental like and dislike of many shrubs. If your garden is on an alkaline soil then there are, unfortunately, many choice and beautiful shrubs which will be difficult or impossible to grow without going to some considerable trouble and expense. Shrubs such as Rhododendrons, Azaleas, Pieris and summer-flowering Heathers need an acid soil provided for them.

This can be achieved most simply by having a raised bed filled with an acid, peaty soil in which you can grow dwarf Rhododendrons, Heathers and other acid-loving plants. This is more effective than making a hole in the ground and filling it with peat, since the plant roots will inevitably get to the side of your pocket and into the alkaline soil beyond, quite apart from infiltration of alkaline water from surrounding soil.

How to change your soil from alkaline to acid

For acid-loving shrubs you would like to grow but cannot fit into a raised bed it will be worth adding flowers of sulphur. This will reduce the pH or alkalinity of your soil when thoroughly dug into the area required. For instance, if you add flowers of sulphur (available at most chemists and garden centres) at a rate of 4 oz. per square yard it should reduce the pH dramatically in one season from 8 to 6·5. But try it on a small area first to prove to yourself that it really works. You will also, of course, have to invest in a soil-testing kit.

How to make a selection

The choice of shrubs available is almost limitless, at least to those who garden on less than two or three acres. Because of their varying sizes and rates of growth it is important to seek advice prior to making your selection. This can be obtained from books, catalogues or direct from nursery or garden centre – at least on the label attached to the plant if not by the resident expert. See what sort of shrubs grow successfully in your neighbours gardens – it will give you a few ideas (though maybe not always the best ones).

Select shrubs carefully, bearing in mind the space available and what you want from your plants – flowers, foliage, fragrance, windbreak, hedge and so on.

Where to buy

Garden centres must be favourite because you can see what you are buying and you can select your own plant. Your shrubs should look healthy and be clearly labelled – the first to give the best chance of establishment, the second so you can look up its likes and dislikes. Specialist nurseries often supply by mail order and you may be able to obtain a wider range from such a source. However, you will need to buy from a reputable company with a name for quality since you cannot see the plants you are purchasing. Beware of cheap offers from mail order companies – you usually get what you pay for! Also beware of many shrubs offered in supermarkets – often they are of poor quality, and success in your garden will not be enhanced by a period of being kept in the wholly artificial environment in a store.

How to make the best use of shrubs in your garden

This book is likely to be a little bit like your garden – too small to get in all the plants one would like to include. Therefore it is essential to try to plan ahead and make the best use of the space available.

In your garden, of course, you may also want annuals, perennials, roses and conifers – which may limit you even more. This is why you need to consider the question of value-for-money shrubs – those that offer not only flower but coloured foliage, good autumn colour and, or course, the possibility of fragrance.

Dwarf shrubs will give you more variety per square metre than such vigorous growers as most Philadelphus, many Cotoneasters, Forsythias and so on. Think of your garden as a year-round feature, and consider form and foliage as well as splashes of colour which many shrubs only provide briefly in the summer months.

Above: In the foreground is Juniperus × media *'Old Gold'; centre:* Berberis thunbergii *'Gold Ring', through which* Clematis montana *spreads happily; beyond:* Syringa palibiniana *in flower*

Foreground: Erica darleyensis *'J. W. Porter'; centre:* Euonymus fortunei *'Emerald 'n Gold' and* Hebe pinguifolia *'Pagei'; back:* Senecio greyi

Planning

You will already have deduced that I suggest careful planning in all garden planting to be a very important factor and the one step most likely to ensure success. At the same time you will be more than a little extraordinary if you do not make some mistakes – I've certainly made my share over the years.

Trees, conifers and shrubs are generally purchased and planted when fairly small – but as we know they don't often stay that way! Most people plant too closely to start with and consequently find that after a few years plants are overcrowded and need thinning out or severe pruning. If you can decide on your main framework planting – those plants that you wish to keep to provide maturity and beauty – before you start planting, then you may save yourself some anguish later. Look up the books or catalogues to get an idea about growth rates and size and try to space accordingly. You can, of course, fill in with other less important but no less attractive shrubs, ground cover or perennials, which can be moved if necessary in later years leaving your more valuable specimens nicely positioned and not too crowded. It is possible to transplant shrubs after a number of years but this can be hard work and success in re-establishment is not always guaranteed.

Planning also incorporates finding the right plant for the right place – sun, shade, good drainage, etc., and here books and catalogues usually give good guidelines, including I hope this slim volume.

Planting

Most shrubs are now sold in pots or containers, though many hedging plants, roses and trees are offered as open-ground bare-root plants. These require the most urgent and careful handling and at no time should the roots be allowed to dry out. If weather or soil conditions are not suitable for planting, either keep them in a cool garage with moist peat around the roots or lay them temporarily into some friable well-drained soil.

It is necessary to prepare your soil thoroughly before planting, clearing perennial weeds completely. It may be necessary to mix peat, leaf-mould or some well-rotted humus to improve the structure of your soil – particularly if it is heavy loam.

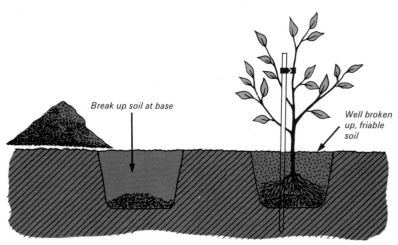

Break up soil at base

Well broken up, friable soil

Planting bare-root plants

Dig your hole to the depth required, making sure to spread the roots out in a natural formation. Stake if necessary and refill, firming well on light land, not too heavily on heavy soils. Water thoroughly if the soil is at all dry.

Planting container plants

Dig your hole as for bare-root plants, then after soaking your pot and rootball thoroughly, drain and carefully remove the pot. If roots are really congested, either prune carefully with secateurs or tease them open. The soil level at the top of the pot should be the same as the eventual ground level. Firm. There will be less necessity for any stake or support for a container plant unless it is a tall shrub or small tree.

Firm in after planting

Pruning

This is a subject on which one could write a book but it will be useful to give at least some guidelines to pruning shrubs.

Needless to say, it is important to have the right tools – a reliable pair of garden shears and sturdy secateurs. A pruning saw is useful for larger branches but is not likely to be essential for most shrubs. Gloves to protect the hands against thorns will be a good investment.

Why prune shrubs?

There are many reasons for pruning shrubs, and without doubt a great many are improved by giving them attention annually, biannually or every few years.

Many shrubs should be pruned every two or three years to prevent them becoming straggly, improve foliage density and flowering performance; Berberis, Euonymus, Hebes, *Potentilla fruticosa*, Hypericums, Santolinas and Spiraeas are examples.

Shrubs grown for foliage or winter stems should be pruned at least every two or three years, almost to the ground. Late winter or early spring is the best time for types such as *Cornus alba* and varieties, *Rubus thibetanus* and others grown for winter stems, Physocarpus and the coloured stemmed Willows (*Salix*).

Spring-flowering shrubs will benefit from pruning back the flowering stems to at least half of their length immediately after flowering. This enables them to make new wood which has time to ripen to produce flowers the following spring.

Generally shrubs which flower during the later part of the summer and autumn, such as Buddleias, Fuchsias, Perovskias, Caryopteris and Ceratostigmas should have their previous year's foliage pruned to within a few inches of the ground in early spring.

Other shrubs need more individual pruning – to shape a choice specimen or to thin out old wood, such as the Hydrangeas, Philadelphus and Deutzias. Many shrubs and some slower-growing trees such as *Populus alba* 'Richardii', *Acer negundo* varieties, or *Salix exigua* can be kept indefinitely as a shrub with annual pruning.

Individual pruning requirements will be given in the following shrub descriptions.

Pruning Sambucus.
Prune in March
with a pruning saw

Pruning Spiraea. ▶
Use secateurs
to prune Spiraea
japonica *types*
in March

◀ **Pruning Buddleia.**
Prune close to the
ground in March
with secateurs

Pruning Lavender. ▶
In March, prune
back with shears.
(See p. 34)

9

A recommended list of shrubs

In a book of this limited size one has naturally to be selective in choosing a list of worthwhile shrubs for the average garden – which is no bad thing. I have tried to select a blend of useful and attractive shrubs, some old, some of recent introduction, some already very popular, some little known. Heights given after descriptions are approximate size after ten years.

Abelia

A range of attractive flowering shrubs for milder localities or for sunny well-drained and sheltered positions in colder areas.

A. 'Francis Mason' is a pretty semi-evergreen with gold and green foliage, scented white flushed pink tubular flowers, June to autumn. 120×120 cm. **A. schumannii** has green leaves flushed red and bell-shaped lilac-pink flowers in late summer. 100×100 cm.

Acer

The Maples fall mostly into the category of trees, but many of the Japanese Maples are suitably dwarf or slow growing to be classed as shrubs and perfect for the small garden where acid or neutral soil exists. Some shade and shelter from cold winds will be needed in early years.

There are many varieties of **A. palmatum** with attractively coloured leaves such as 'Atropurpureum' and 'Bloodgood', both reddish purple all summer, 'Butterfly', variegated, and 'Aureum', golden leaved. The cut-leaf maples **A. p. 'Dissectum'** and varieties are perfect for the rock or peat garden. Look for **A. p. 'Dissectum Garnet'**, or 'Inabashidare', both purple.

Top left: Acer japonicum *'Aureum'*
Bottom left: Acer negundo *'Flamingo'*
Below: Andromeda polifolia *'Compacta'*

Top left: Berberis darwinii
Left: Berberis thunbergii *'Rose Glow'*
Above: Berberis thunbergii *'Bagatelle'*

One of the slowest but possibly most striking is **A. japonicum 'Aureum'**. Most are propagated by grafting, so expect them to be expensive. **A. negundo 'Elegans'**, **'Variegatum'** and **'Flamingo'** have brightly coloured leaves and are easier, and, though all will make small trees if left, can with regular pruning be maintained as shrubs to spectacular effect.

Andromeda

A small group of low-growing acid-loving evergreen shrubs, preferring moist, peaty soils.

One of the prettiest and most reliable is **A. polifolia 'Compacta'** with silvery-blue leaves and masses of pearly-pink bell flowers in May and June. 15 cm.

Aucuba

This family of evergreen Laurel-like shrubs are adaptable to sun or shade and even quite inhospitable sites. Golden-leaved and variegated forms will need full sun to bring out their often startling colours. They come in both male and female forms; the latter produces berries only when a male form is planted near by. So when purchasing make sure you get both sexes if you want to be sure of berries.

Berberis

The Barberries are among the most popular of shrubs and the family contains a very wide range indeed, from dwarf to tall, deciduous to evergreen, flowering to foliage. Most are completely hardy and generally of easy cultivation for sun or part shade. Many benefit from hard pruning every few years, but since some have vicious thorns make sure to wear a thick pair of leather gloves.

B. darwinii. Discovered in Chile by Charles Darwin in 1835, this has dark green leaves and drooping racemes of beautiful orange-yellow flowers in April and May, often followed by purple berries in autumn. 150–200 cm.

B. rubrostilla and its many varieties are fine where space permits. Deciduous with very thorny stems, most have coral-red berries in autumn, remaining after leaf fall. 90–120 cm.

B. stenophylla is a popular evergreen species though eventually becoming quite large. Green leaves, prickly stems which are gracefully pendulous and covered with golden-yellow flowers in April or May. Both the species and *B. s.* 'Claret Cascade' with maroon stems and leaves make excellent hedges. 180–200 cm in ten years. *B. s.* 'Corallina Compacta' is a dwarf shrub of great merit with glossy green leaves and orange-yellow flowers in May and sometimes in autumn. 40×50 cm.

B. thunbergii. This deciduous species has given rise to some excellent garden cultivars, grown primarily for their foliage since they seldom flower. *B. t.* 'Aurea' has beautiful clear yellow leaves, not difficult but best in a sheltered and part shady position. *B. t.* 'Atropurpurea Nana' is first class as a dwarf shrub with dark purple foliage, but to my mind now surpassed by the more compact *B. t.* 'Bagatelle' with leaves a brighter coppery red. Both 30–40 cm. *B. t.* 'Helmond Pillar' is distinct in its narrow erect habit and deep purple leaves. 75–100 cm. *B. t.* 'Rose Glow' makes a colourful shrub with purple leaves and new shoots and foliage brightly splashed with pink and cream. 100 cm. Prune hard every three or four years. Lastly *B. t.* 'Silver Beauty' with light green leaves and new shoots suffused silvery white and pink provides an excellent contrast with good autumn colour, too. 75–100 cm.

Buddleia

Known as the Butterfly Bush, these popular and invaluable shrubs undoubtedly live up to their name, attracting butterflies on summer days. All prefer a well-drained sunny situation, but will prosper on heavier soils too.

B. alternifolia with narrow dark green leaves and the silvery-leaved *B. a.* 'Argentea' both become large shrubs in time. Long arching branches and scented flowers in June and July. Prune after flowering. 180–200 cm. The species *B. davidii* has produced a wide range of showy garden varieties with large grey-green, silvery or variegated leaves and panicles of flowers in late summer. These can be pink, red, blue, purple and white and all will benefit from an annual hard pruning in March. 200 cm.

B. nanhoensis. A dwarfer species with a bushy habit and slender arching stems. Look for *B. n.* 'Nanho Blue' and *B. n.* 'Nanho Purple', both excellent garden shrubs. Prune hard in March 120–150 cm.

Buxus

Evergreen shrubs which are seldom seen these days except in old, often more formal gardens. Slow growing but not fussy as to soils and good plants for edging. Some with variegated foliage are attractive in their own right. Though most have latinised names, they are generally all forms of B. sempervirens, the Common Box.

Callicarpa

A small group of easily grown shrubs adaptable to sun or part shade, useful for their bright show of berries in autumn and winter.

C. bodinieri 'Profusion' is outstanding for the many clusters of shiny lilac-purple berries it bears each autumn. 125 cm.

Buddleia nanhoensis *'Nanho Purple'*

Caryopteris clandonensis

C. bodinieri *'Profusion'*

Camellia *'Donation'*

Calluna

The Heather or Ling. There is now such a tremendous range of these ornamental shrubs for the garden that together with the Erica family or Heaths they form the basis of a book in this series devoted to them and their uses. Callunas can, of course, be used among other shrubs but require an acid soil and prefer a sunny situation.

Camellia

Superb evergreen shrubs deserving a wider use. Hardy in the UK, except in exceptionally severe winters or exposed situations, they require neutral or acid soil. Try them in tubs, raised beds or containers if your soil isn't right. Ideal in a light woodland shade and also in a south-, west- or even north-facing wall position where the flowers can be protected from the early morning sun during periods of spring frosts. Depending on which part of the UK you live in and the variety, flowers start to open from late winter and can carry on until late spring. Innumerable varieties exist with quite exotic forms and colour combinations, from brightest red, through pink, to white and even yellow, with both single and double flowers anything up to 15 cm across.

Caryopteris

These are very pretty low growing shrubs for a sunny well-drained position, with grey-green aromatic leaves and spikes carrying abundant bright blue flowers in late summer and autumn. The species generally offered is C. clandonensis, *with a variety, 'Heavenly Blue', being equally attractive with slightly deeper blue flowers. 75–90 cm. Prune old stems hard to the ground in March.*

Ceanothus *'Puget Blue'* Choisya ternata

Ceanothus

Both deciduous and evergreen shrubs, many classed as tender except in sunny, well-sheltered positions. The evergreens are the least hardy, but many are ideal used as wall shrubs or climbers, though some training will be required.

C. **'Cascade'** with clusters of blue flowers in early spring is excellent for this purpose though **'Autumnal Blue'** is somewhat hardier. **'Blue Mound'** and the lower growing *C. thyrsiflorus* **'Repens'** make compact bushes flowering freely in summer as does the taller, small-leaved **'Puget Blue'** – all reasonably hardy in the British Isles in fairly sheltered positions. The most popular deciduous forms are **'Gloire de Versailles'**, powder-blue clusters, **'Topaz'** indigo-blue and **'Marie Simon'**, a less common pink.

Deciduous varieties settle happily among other shrubs in sheltered positions. Prune these lightly as new shoots appear in early spring, while evergreens are best trimmed immediately after flowering.

Ceratostigma

Low-growing shrubs for sunny well-drained positions and useful for late show of blue flowers.

The most popular is the invaluable *C. willmottianum*, making a dense twiggy bush up to 75 cm with fluffy heads of deepest blue from July until autumn. Prune to the ground each March.

Chaenomeles

Also known as Japonica, the Japanese Quince are useful hardy shrubs, both in the border, for ground cover, or trained against a wall. A great number of varieties are in cultivation, often with spectacular flowers which appear in early spring just prior or during appearance of the first leaves. Often flowers are followed by large golden-yellow fruits which can be used to make jelly. They can make untidy shrubs but pruning can be carried out immediately after flowering – beware of thorns!

There are a great many varieties of both *C. speciosa* and *C. superba*, most flowering freely year after year in sun or part shade, and on almost any soil. In the former species try **'Brilliant'**, a bright scarlet, **'Nivalis'**, pure white, or **'Umbilicata'**, deep salmon-pink; while among varieties of *C. superba* look for the startling and ever popular **'Crimson and Gold'** (see front cover), **'Nicolene'**, a scarlet red, or **'Pink Lady'** which has large deep pink flowers. Habits vary somewhat with some more spreading than others, with possible size at ten years estimated at 100–150 cm by as much across.

Chimonanthus

Known as Wintersweet because of its beautifully fragrant flowers in midwinter.

The more common of the two species is **C. fragrans**, an easily grown deciduous shrub best situated in a sunny well-drained position where its wood will ripen to produce yellow, purple-centred flowers from November until February, though only on well-established plants. Good for cutting, and this will probably provide enough pruning requirements to maintain a bushy habit. 120–150 cm.

Choisya ternata

The Mexican Orange Blossom is an extremely popular garden plant and hardier than the name suggests. As easy shrub for well-drained soil in sun or part shade. It makes a mound of bright green glossy leaves above which large clusters of deliciously fragrant white flowers appear in April and May and often at later times during the summer. Though not usually necessary it will take kindly to pruning after flowering, or earlier in spring if damaged by winter snows, breaking freely into new growth from the base. 120–150 cm.

Cistus

A family of sun-loving shrubs related to the Helianthemums or Rock Roses. Though bright and attractive in flower few can be considered hardy enough, except in warm and sheltered districts of Britain, to withstand severe winters. Most flower between late May and July, with heights varying between 30 cm and 120 cm. Plant in a sunny well-drained position for best results.

Cornus

Collectively known as Cornels or Dogwoods, this group of small deciduous trees and shrubs provide foliage, flower, and in winter many reward with brightly coloured stems. Most are of easy cultivation, with C. alba and C. stolonifera forms revelling in damp boggy situations as well as light sandy soils.

C. alba, the Red-barked Dogwood, has attractive red stems in winter and has given us some good garden forms that also have attractive foliage. Prune hard in March or

Left: Cornus alba *'Aurea'; right:* Cornus alternifolia *'Argentea'*

April at least every other year to retain compactness and get best winter colour from stems. Without pruning most varieties will reach 200–250 cm.

C. a. '**Aurea**' has soft golden-yellow leaves, *C. a.* '**Variegata**' (also known as *C. a.* '**Elegantissima**') has grey-green and white leaves. Similar but more compact with dark green margined white leaves is *C. a.* '**Sibirica Variegata**'. *C. a.* '**Sibrica**' itself, the Westonbirt Dogwood, has the brightest red winter stems of all. *C. a.* '**Spaethii**' is quite different with golden variegated leaves.

The greeny-yellow-stemmed *C. stolonifera* '**Flaviramea**' is closely related to *C. alba* and requiring similar treatment. A much dwarfer form with attractively veined green leaves is *C. s.* '**Kelsey**' which makes excellent ground cover. 40–50 cm.

C. alternifolia '**Variegata**', also known as *C. a.* '**Argentea**', makes a superb shrub or small tree in a sheltered spot. Tiered branches with small silvery-white variegated leaves make a bright show all summer. 250–300 cm.

There are many other excellent Dogwoods which are slow growing enough to be classed as shrubs, though eventually making small trees. The following thrive best on acid or neutral soils.

C. florida, the North American flowering Dogwood, produces petal-like bracts on mature plants in red, white and pink, and good autumn colour, while *C. kousa* and *C. kousa chinensis*, both with creamy-white bracts, from Japan and China make magnificent specimens where some shade and good soil exists. *C. mas*, the Cornelian Cherry, has bright yellow flowers on bare winter stems, but get the best of both worlds by looking for those with coloured foliage such as *C. m.* '**Aurea**' with golden-yellow leaves, *C. m.* '**Elegantissima**', cream, yellow and pink, and brightest of all *C. m.* '**Variegata**' with silvery-white leaves. The foliage forms may need a sheltered position until well established but are otherwise not difficult.

Corylus maxima *'Purpurea'*   Cotinus coggygria *'Royal Purple'*

C. dammeri 'Coral Beauty' · Cotoneaster 'Exburiensis'

Corylopsis

Related to the Witch Hazels this small group of shrubs need a position sheltered from spring frosts, providing attractive mostly fragrant pendant yellow flowers in early spring. Most though low growing eventually make quite large shrubs which can be pruned after flowering if required. Though adaptable to other types, acid or neutral soils seem preferred.

Corylus

A range of trees and shrubs most commonly grown for their fruits or nuts, but which contain a few worthwhile shrubs or small trees. Most are easily grown on any soil and the three mentioned can be pruned hard back every few years if required to be kept as a shrub. This is best done in late winter.

C. avellana 'Aurea'. A golden-leaved form of Hazel. Long catkins in early spring before leaves appear, the leaves remaining a bright golden yellow all summer. 200–300 cm. **C. a.** 'Contorta', the Corkscrew Hazel, has curiously twisted and contorted stems from which catkins hang in early spring. More attractive in winter than summer. Cut out any suckers which may occur at the base as soon as seen. 200 cm. **C. maxima** 'Purpurea', the Purple-leaved Filbert, is a useful foliage shrub and a perfect contrast to **C. a.** 'Aurea'. Vigorous habit with broad deep purple leaves, it also has purple catkins though often shy in producing them. 200 cm.

Cotinus

Until recently known as Rhus cotinus, *and still commonly as the Smoke Tree. This small range of shrubs prefer a sunny spot on well-drained soils. New leaves seldom appear until well into May and on the most ornamental garden forms these are a striking purple.*

C. coggygria 'Royal Purple' is the most notable, making an eventually large shrub of intense deep purple all season. Site carefully against contrasting shrubs or plants. Fluffy pinkish-red flower heads will appear in June or July on mature plants, fading to a smoky grey by August. Prune as required in April to maintain size required and more compact habit. 200–300 cm.

Cotoneaster

A vast family of shrubs, some dwarf, some of tree-like proportions and a great many of great garden value, in fact one could claim there is a Cotoneaster for almost every soil

17

and situation. Most have white flowers in summer followed by fruits of various colours, unfortunately often as attractive to birds as to us gardeners!

All are relatively easy to grow and will withstand heavy pruning as and when necessary. Below is a selection of some of the best garden forms.

LOW GROWING FORMS

C. congestus is a dwarf creeping evergreen with tiny rounded leaves, ideal for hanging over a wall or low ground cover. Seldom fruits. 15 cm. *C. dammeri*, also evergreen, is much more vigorous and ideal for ground cover, making an extremely flat carpet with red fruits in late summer. 15 cm. *C. d.* **'Coral Beauty'** is less prostrate to 50 cm with smaller dark green leaves and an abundance of coral-red fruits in autumn. The popular *C. horizontalis* is a deciduous shrub and though normally prostrate is seen more often trained up a wall where it can be most effective with its 'herringbone' pattern of branching smothered in bright red berries in autumn. The slower growing *C. h.* **'Variegata'** is a first-class shrub in its own right, slower growing with leaves edged creamy white. 30–40 cm. *C. m. thymifolius* is a distinctive dwarf shrub with glossy green leaves and a congested spiky habit.

MEDIUM TO TALL GROWING FORMS

C. bullatus is a handsome deciduous form, large leaves turning scarlet in autumn and vying with clusters of crimson berries. 200 cm. *C. cornubia* is an evergreen shrub of almost tree-like proportions and ideal for screening. Large green leaves, white flowers and masses of red fruits in autumn. Of similar habit is the hybrid *C.* **'Exburiensis'** with yellow berries. Both 300–400 cm. There are many medium growers excellent for banks or ground cover; try the evergreen *C. conspicuus*, broad spreading habit and red berries, or the lower growing *C. c.* **'Decorus'** which is equally useful. *C. microphyllus* is also evergreen with small leaves and solitary scarlet berries in autumn. 80–100 cm.

Lastly one should mention *C.* **'Hybridus Pendulus'**, the dual-purpose shrub. Normally a fairly vigorous spreading semi-evergreen, but trained up a stem it makes an effective small tree, with branches smothered each autumn with shiny red berries, cascading downwards in a graceful fashion.

Cotoneaster *'Hybridus Pendulus'*   Cytisus kewensis

Cytisus

The Brooms are an invaluable group of shrubs and though usually brief in flower and sometimes short in their lifespan provide an amazing range of colourful flowers during May and June. Generally adaptable to most soils but succeeding best with sun, good drainage and acid or neutral rather than highly alkaline soils.

Pruning is best carried out immediately after flowering to prevent plants becoming leggy. It is not possible to list all the varieties here but a short list of various types may be helpful.

C. beanii is a dwarf spreading form to 30 cm with deep golden-yellow flowers in April and May, but perhaps the most striking prostrate variety is *C. kewensis* whose sparse branches are transformed in May when smothered by masses of cream-coloured flowers. *C. praecox* is a popular Broom growing to about 150 cm, with rich cream flowers almost weighing down the foliage in May. Similar but white is *C. p. albus*, while the dwafer *C. p.* 'Allgold' is golden yellow. 120 cm.

Of the garden hybrids look for such varieties as **'Burkwoodii'**, cerise and crimson; **'Dukaat'**, compact gold and yellow; *C.* **'Hollandia'**, cream and purple; **'Killiney Red'**, deep red; **'Lena'**, a striking compact shrub with yellow and red flowers; **'Moonlight'**, sulphur-yellow; **'Windlesham Ruby'**, carmine-red; and **'Zeelandia'**, a creamy pink.

Many varieties also exist of the species *C. scoparius*, the Common Broom, with an equally wide range of colours. Most reach 150–200 cm.

Daphne

The Daphnes are among the most desirable of shrubs and particularly noted for their often sweetly fragrant flowers. Though there is a wide range of shapes and sizes in cultivation, in reality many are hard to come by, primarily because they are not the most reliable to grow successfully in nurseries or in gardens. They generally require a reasonably good but well-drained soil which at the same time doesn't dry out too much.

Most garden centres will stock a few varieties, but for the wider range of dwarfer types you will need to look for the specialists.

Deutzia

A large family of easily grown deciduous shrubs related to Philadelphus and suited to most garden soils where not too dry. The range of colours is limited to pink and white but some of them are quite beautiful when in flower in June. Prune flowering stems immediately after flowering has finished, and congested old wood can be thinned to the base of the plant at the same time or in late winter.

The dwarf to medium growing forms are perhaps the most useful for modern gardens. *D. chunii*, for instance, a shrub of broad spreading habit, has large pink white-centred flowers in July. At 100 cm this is only slightly larger than *D. rosea* 'Carminea', a superb shrub with arching branches smothered in May and June with flowers of carmine-pink fading to light pink. Slightly dwarfer still is *D. elegantissima* 'Rosealind' with deep rose-pink flowers in June lasting for some weeks, and *D. compacta* 'Lavender Time'. The latter makes a bushy shrub to 75 cm with lightly scented flowers of pale lilac in June fading to white during warm sunshine.

Above: Cytisus *'Lena'* is a striking
dwarf Broom, shown in full flower in
May
Right: Deutzia elegantissima *'Rosealind'*
is an easy shrub, providing masses of
flowers in June

Larger are **D. magnifica** with large clusters of double white flowers and **D. 'Montrose'**, a popular hybrid of bushy habit with mauve-pink flowers. Both grow to 200 cm and flower in June.

More vigorous to 300 cm are **D. scabra** and its cultivars. **D. scabra** has large clusters of pure white flowers perhaps surpassed by the double form **D. s. 'Plena'** whose flowers are flushed pink.

Diervilla

A genus of only three species of shrubs sometimes confused with the better known Weigelas, but actually related to the Honeysuckle.

Though little known and seldom offered I believe the species **D. splendens** to be among the best of garden shrubs. It is deciduous, with leaves of light yellow-green deepening as summer progresses with shades of green and bronze and attractively veined. Small tubular yellow flowers enhance from June to late summer. Easy growing and inclined to sucker. Prune hard back in late winter just before new growth appears. 75–100 cm.

Elaeagnus

Useful shrubs for foliage effect and in particular the cultivars of the evergreen species E. pungens and E. ebbingei. They are generally adaptable to most soils and localities in Britain, succeeding well in coastal districts. For hedging purposes they are best pruned in June and September, but harder pruning if required should be done in early May before new growth starts. Variegated forms often tend to revert to green and these shoots should be pruned out as soon as seen.

E. ebbingei is a fast growing hybrid species with large shiny green leaves which are silvery beneath. Fragrant scaly-white flowers appear (in the autumn) where the leaves join the stems. 300 cm. There is an attractive variety called **E. e. 'Limelight'** which has a central splash of green on the leaves with irregular greenish-yellow rims. **E. e. 'Gilt Edge'** is equally attractive with bright golden-yellow and green leaves. **E. pungens.** There are many variegated forms of this species which make a bright show, being particularly noticeable in winter. **E. p. 'Maculata'** is the best known, making a large bushy shrub with quite thorny stems. Glossy green leaves have golden-yellow centres and green surrounds. **E. m. 'Goldrim'** is very similar but green in the centre of the leaf and edged with gold. 200 cm.

Diervilla splendens

Elaeagnus pungens *'Maculata'*

Enkianthus

This group of acid-loving shrubs is worth at least a brief mention, if only because they give not only attractive pendulous bell-shaped flowers in spring but excellent autumn leaf colour. Slow growing, with some species having yellow to red flowers, some dwarf in habit and others eventually 200 cm or more. Look for E. campanulatus *and* E. chinensis.

Above: A view of the author's garden in March shows the variety of form and colour that can be achieved using mainly conifers and heathers for year-round effect. Winter-flowering Ericas are in full flower and further colour is provided by the foliage of summer-flowering types. In the foreground can be seen Erica carnea 'Pink Spangles', while Erica carnea 'Springwood White' can be seen in the distance. Shrubs such as the dwarf purple-leaved Berberis, Euonymus fortunei, and Potentilla fruticosa can be mixed in to create even more variety. The scene above can, of course, be adapted for the smaller garden using groups of three heathers or even less

Escallonia *'Red Elf'*

Euonymus europaea *'Red Cascade'*

Erica

The Heaths are covered in my book in this series, Heaths and Heathers, *but worth drawing to attention here as superb shrubs which can be mixed in with others to supply both winter and summer flowers and colourful foliage.*

Remember winter-flowering species such as **E. carnea**, **E. erigena** and the Tree Heaths will tolerate lime, while the summer-flowering **E. cinerea**, **E. ciliaris**, **E. tetralix** and **E. vagans** must have an acid soil. Prune summer-flowering varieties in March, winter flowering (if necessary at all) as flowers fade in April or early May.

Escallonia

A large and important range of flowering shrubs, though some are hardier than others and in severe winters one would expect them to be cut to the ground, though seldom killed outright if planted in a sunny well-drained position. Ideal for seaside plantings, where they are often used as hedge or windbreaks. Generally they have small leaves and quite small flowers, but in a mass can be extremely showy. These start often in June and continue until late summer or early autumn. Some species and varieties are deciduous while others could be considered evergreen, but this often depends upon location.

Pruning can be carried out in a tidying-up fashion in August, cutting back flowering shoots by half to make a bushier plant, or more severely in late spring. Heights may vary from 60 cm to 200 cm. Since there are so many, often similar varieties I will mention only a few distinct and popular ones.

E. 'Apple Blossom' is a medium-sized shrub with quite large pink and white flowers; **'Crimson Spire'**, vigorous in growth, bright crimson; **'Donard Seedling'**, flesh-pink in bud, opening white; **'Gwendolyn Anley'**, a hardy dwarfer shrub to 100 cm with masses of small pink flowers; **'Red Elf'**, an excellent dwarf red with dark glossy green leaves; **E. rubra 'Woodside'**, a deciduous low growing shrub with small crimson flowers. 60 cm.

Euonymus

A family containing both small trees and low growing foliage shrubs, both extremely attractive and useful as garden plants and both adaptable to a wide range of conditions including chalky soils. The tree forms will probably require little or no pruning but the forms of E. fortunei *and* E. japonica *will often benefit from an annual trim with shears in late winter.*

E. europaea 'Red Cascade'. This selection from our native Spindle Bush makes a large shrub or small tree with leaves giving autumn colour, but it is most striking when these drop to expose the masses of pendulous coral-red fruits which almost weigh the tree down in early autumn. 250 cm. **E. fortunei.** This species contains many worthwhile dwarf ground-covering shrubs, all with small oval-shaped leaves. **E. f. 'Dart's Blanket'** is perhaps the best green-leaved form and excellent for ground cover, only 30–40 cm in height; **E. f. 'Emerald Gaiety'** has bright white and green variegated leaves, more bushy to 75 cm, while **E. f. 'Emerald 'n Gold'** is deservedly popular as a year-round foliage shrub of similar height but with gold and green variegations. **E. f. 'Sunspot'** is quite different with dark green leaves splashed with a golden-yellow centre. **E. f. 'Minimus'** has minute green leaves, veined silver and perfect for the rock-garden. All of these can be used as wall shrubs against which they will happily climb, though **E. f. 'Variegata'** might be considered the best for this purpose. **E. japonica** is of a more erect bushy habit with larger leaves and has produced a great many brightly coloured foliage forms which need full sun for best effect. **E. j. 'Ovatus Aureus'** is the most popular of these with both pure gold and golden variegated leaves – almost too bright for my liking! 100 cm.

Exochorda

All the species in this genus are deciduous and have white flowers in May. Most make quite large, rather untidy bushes gradually building up to a mounded specimen with drooping branches, and spectacular flowers.

Plant them on their own in a shrub border in an open sunny situation on any soil that is not highly alkaline. If necessary prune long stems back immediately after flowering.

E. macrantha 'The Bride' is perhaps the best garden variety with a relatively compact habit and such a mass of snow-white flowers that for a short time the stems can hardly be seen. 125 cm.

E. fortunei *'Emerald 'n Gold'*

Exochorda macrantha *'The Bride'*

Forsythia intermedia

Fuchsia *'Tom Thumb'*

Forsythia

Almost the most universal, hardiest and easiest shrub to grow but, though common, indispensable for its early spring display when little else is in flower. There are many species and even more varieties in cultivation, but all should be pruned back to old wood immediately after flowering to enable the plant to produce new growth for next year's flowers. Many varieties will grow to 3 m or more unless regularly pruned.

Look for **F. 'Beatrix Farrand'**, with large canary-yellow flowers; **F. *intermedia* 'Minigold'**, dwarfer to 150 cm but with large flowers; **F. *i.* 'Spectabilis'**, one of the freest to flower; **F. *i.* 'Lynwood'**, another vigorous free flowering form with large rich yellow flowers; **F. *ovata***, an earlier flowering species from Korea, scented yellow flowers on compact bushes; and lastly a dwarf form in **F. *viridissima* 'Bronxensis'**, which reaches only to 40 cm and if it were freer to flower would make a first-class dwarf shrub.

Fothergilla

Related to the Witch Hazels, these are attractive if little-known shrubs requiring acid or neutral soil. They are slow growing, preferring sun or part shade. Fragrant white bottle-brush flowers appear in April and May before the green leaves unfurl, themselves providing often a marvellous show of colour in the autumn.

F. *gardenii* is dwarf, growing to less than 100 cm, though similar in most respects in flower and foliage to **F. *major***, which may reach 200 cm.

Fuchsia

These shrubs have achieved such popularity in recent years that they are worth a volume on their own. There are such a multitude of varieties available with pendant flowers of varying sizes and colour combinations, though certainly not all could be classed as fully hardy. But the hardy types are excellent value and even if cut to the ground by frost each winter, they will grow again to provide a succession of flowers from midsummer onwards. They will grow on most soils but are best where good drainage exists, though in summer they will be happier if kept well watered. Pruning consists only of removing last year's dead stems in early spring before new shoots begin. There exists a good range of species and varieties, the stronger forms reaching perhaps 200 cm in coastal or warmer districts where they are semi-evergreen, but half of that height when growing from ground level. At the other end of the scale some dwarfer forms may only reach 30–40 cm.

For a taller hardy variety try *F.* '**Riccartoni**', popular as hedging in coastal districts and with smaller red and purple flowers than '**Mrs Popple**', which is likely to remain between 60–100 cm. *F. magellanica* '**Aurea**' is a marvellous foliage shrub with small red flowers and bright golden-yellow leaves and there is a variegated form, too, though this is not quite so hardy. For a real dwarf try '**Tom Thumb**', which grows only to 30–40 cm and a succession of red and purple flowers.

Garrya

A genus of evergreen shrubs adaptable to most soils but unfortunately not completely hardy in all locations. Best where some shelter can be given from strong and cold winds, and excellent grown under the protection of a wall, particularly if south or west facing. It is given the name of the Silk Tassel Bush.

The most generally offered species is *G. elliptica*, but only the male form has the long tassel-like flowers. These are greyish green and appear in late winter against the dark green foliage and can be as much as 25 cm in length. A more vigorous form is *G. elliptica* '**James Roof**', with even longer catkins.

The stems can be cut for winter decoration, but since your specimen might eventually reach 300 cm by as much across, some other pruning might also be necessary and this should be done in April.

Gaultheria

A family of dwarf, creeping, acid-loving shrubs closely related to Vacciniums. They prefer peaty, reasonably moist soils in part or full shade but will also succeed in sun where not too dry, spreading by underground runners. Normally they have small bell-shaped flowers in late spring and early summer, followed by attractive coloured fruits.

G. procumbens is the best-known form with large red fruits lasting all winter and only 15 cm high, while *G. miqueliana* is not much taller, providing an alternative with white fruits, though the dense green foliage often hides them. There are several other species sometimes offered by nurserymen.

Garrya elliptica

Gaultheria procumbens

Genista pilosa 'Lemon Spreader'   Mamamelis mollis 'Pallida'

Genista

This group of shrubs is closely allied to Cytisus and many species share the same common name of Broom. They are mostly low growing, preferring open sunny positions and well-drained soils where they can be relied upon to flower freely around May each year. All have pea-like flowers in various shades of yellow. Not all types will need pruning but if required do so immediately after flowering – best not into old wood.

G. hispanica. The Spanish Gorse is an excellent dwarf shrub to about 60 cm, with spiny congested branches and smothered in deep yellow flowers each May. **G. lydia** is another first-class shrub with a twiggy semi-prostrate habit becoming a sheet of golden yellow in early summer before new growth begins. It can become open and untidy with age so trimming is advisable. **G. pilosa** is a completely prostrate form with small green leaves. Ideal for ground cover or to hang over a wall and only 15 cm high. Similar but with larger deeper yellow flowers is **G. p. 'Lemon Spreader'**.

Hamamelis

The Witch Hazels are among the choicest and most sought after of shrubs, not always easy to come by and expensive because they must be propagated by grafting. Why? Because they are such marvellous winter-flowering shrubs, with clusters of often sweetly scented flowers cheering up the winter – and usually providing a show in the autumn with brightly coloured leaves. Best in a reasonably open position in all but thin chalk soils, and worth siting against a background where winter flowers will stand out. Add ample peat or leaf mould when planting followed by an annual mulch of the same material.

The flowers come in shades of yellow, through orange and to red. Look for **H. mollis**, the Chinese Witch Hazel, with golden-yellow flowers; the incomparable **H. mollis 'Pallida'**, a bright clear yellow and very fragrant; **H×intermedia 'Jelena'** or **'Copper Beauty'**, yellow flushed coppery red; and lastly **H. ×i. 'Diane'**, the best and deepest red. But don't necessarily turn down others of almost equal merit! Eventually as high as 3 m and as broad, it may be advisable to take corrective pruning if space becomes restricted, this best in March or April.

Hebe

A large family of evergreen shrubs mostly originating from New Zealand, some minute in habit and suitable for the rock garden, others for ground cover and foliage, and the

Hebe ochracea *'James Stirling'*   Hebe *'Quicksilver'*

larger types make good summer- and autumn-flowering shrubs, thriving particularly well near coastal districts. Dwarfer forms are generally hardier and flower in spring or summer.

Hebes mostly require a well-drained soil and though tolerating shade prefer full sun. Many, and particularly the taller varieties, are on the borderline of hardiness in colder parts of Britain. Pruning may be necessary on those damaged or cut back by frost or to keep them more bushy and compact in habit. This is best done in April.

The 'whipcord' varieties are perhaps the hardiest and look more like conifers: **H. armstrongii**, with a spreading habit, bronze foliage and dainty white flowers in spring; **H. cupressoides**, similar but narrower greyish-green branches to 75 cm, **H. c. 'Golden Dome'** being a more compact form with conspicuous golden leaves the year round, and **H. ochracea 'James Stirling'** a superb compact form to only 25 cm, green in summer and bronze in winter.

H. pinguifolia 'Pagei' is a popular dwarf shrub to 15 cm with small blue-grey leaves and white flowers in spring, an excellent dwarf shrub on the rock garden or for ground cover. **H. rakaeinsis (syn. H. subalpina)** has a similar habit though reaching 45 cm, and with bright green leaves and white flowers. **H. 'Quicksilver'** is a recent introduction with bright silver-blue leaves and a twiggy prostrate habit. In the taller varieties there is **H. andersonii 'Variegata'**, 100 cm, with lavender-blue flowers and white variegated foliage; **H. brachysiphon (syn. H. traversii)**, 150 cm, with green leaves and small white flowers, which has a dwarfer form called **'White Gem'** growing to only 60 cm; **H. speciosa 'La Seduisante' (syn. H. 'Diamant')**, 120 cm, with bright crimson flowers; and **'Mrs Winder'**, 100 cm, with purple leaves and bright blue flowers.

Hedera

Though 'the ivies' are normally classed as climbers, many are very effective used as ground cover or for trailing over walls, banks or climbing over stumps. Generally speaking as garden shrubs they require good drainage, growing well in sun but perhaps even more successfully in shade. Some trimming may be needed to keep certain varieties in check.

There are large-leaved forms, **_H. colchica_** and varieties and the smaller leaved Common Ivy **_H. helix_**. Among the latter is as great a variation in leaf and colour as one would wish to find, some much hardier than others. Many have been adapted for use as evergreen house plants and, of course, in hanging baskets.

Helianthemum

The Rock Roses are normally listed among alpines and a full list is included in the Alpine book in this series. However, they are strictly speaking shrubs and can be used as edging plants or for frontal positions in the shrub border as well as on the rock garden. Best in a sunny well-drained position where they will live happily for some years, but if inclined to untidiness trim hard back in March or April and new shoots will appear from the base. Otherwise trim lightly with shears after flowering. A wide range of colours can be found among the innumerable varieties, most of which are reliably evergreen and flower in May and June.

Helichrysum

Both shrubby and alpine plants are found in this genus, the shrubs tending to have silver or grey aromatic leaves and yellow flowers, requiring sunny well-drained positions where they can be expected to survive most British winters.

Hibiscus

Deciduous shrubs of considerable attraction with large Hollyhock-like flowers in a wide range of colours. These are large and trumpet shaped, normally giving of their best in warm sheltered positions and in hot summers and then flowering in succession from July to October. Though many if left unpruned might grow as high as 3 m they will flower on new season's growth if pruned hard in March or April, but flowers may begin later.

The best plants for Britain are forms of **_H. syriacus_**, most of which are slow growing though eventually they may reach 250 cm. A few recommended cultivars are: **_H. s._ 'Blue Bird'**, violet-blue with a violet eye; **_H. s._ 'Hamabo'**, large single pink with a crimson centre; **_H. s._ 'Pink Giant'**, large deep single pink and a deeper coloured centre; the striking **_H. s._ 'Red Heart'**, white with a red centre; **_H. s._ 'Woodbridge'**, a single deep red; and both **_H. s._ 'W. R. Smith'** and **_H. s._ 'Diane'**, are striking single whites. The singles seem to succeed best in our northerly climate but the doubles can be equally attractive where grown well.

Hedera helix *'Gold Heart'*

Hibiscus syriacus *'Pink Giant'*

Hydrangea

The Hydrangeas are universally popular both as hardy garden shrubs and as pot plants for the home.

There is a very wide range of hardy varieties for gardeners to choose from, some with quite spectacular heads of flowers. These appear on all species and varieties from late June or after and provide a show of colour right through until autumn, particularly where they receive adequate moisture. All like good rich soil, will grow in sun or part shade with ample water but flowering stems can be damaged by heavy winter and particularly spring frosts. Except for one or two species the only pruning required is to remove in spring the previous year's dead flower heads and any untidy or very old woody stems. Plants become more resistant to frost as they mature, though a mulch of peat, leaf-mould or composted manure before winter will assist in protection.

H. macrophylla, a species from Japan, has given us most of the best garden varieties and these Lacecaps are the most natural forms, with small bluish fertile flowers surrounded by large showy flattened sterile ray 'florets'. The blue-flowered cultivars will need an acid soil to retain that colour, otherwise they will be pink or lilac. *H. m.* **'Blue Wave'** is recommended, and an attractive counterpart is **'White Wave'**, with white florets, both reach about 100 cm.

The other types which come under *H. macrophylla* are known as Hortensias and these are called 'Mop Heads' for their more rounded heads of fully sterile flowers. There are many varieties, but one might mention **'Altona'**, rose coloured; **'Ami Pasquier'**, dwarfish red; **'Mme E. Mouillière'**, the best white; and **'Générale Vicomtesse de Vibraye'**, pink but sky-blue on acid soils. *H. paniculata* **'Grandiflora'**, **'Praecox'** and **'Tardiva'** are all worthwhile larger shrubs with large pyramidal heads of white, later flushed pink flowers. *H.* **'Preziosa'** is one of the finest of recent introductions, with green leaves which turn reddish bronze in late summer, and has masses of pink flower heads in June and July, turning to reddish purple as summer progresses. 120 cm. *H. serrata* has given some good forms with compact growth to about 100 cm, similar to the Lacecaps but with smaller flattened sterile flower heads. Look for the beautiful *H. s.* **'Bluebird'** and *H. s.* **'Grayswood'**.

Hydrangea *'Preziosa'*

Hydrangea paniculata *'Tardiva'*

Top left: Hypericum indorum 'Hysan'
Bottom left: Hypericum prolificum
Below: Ilex ferox 'Argentea'

Hypericum

*An extremely useful family of mostly deciduous shrubs, varying in size from 10 cm –
these classed among alpine shrubs – to 200 cm, and all with yellow flowers.*

*They are normally free flowering, often making a show from early summer until
autumn, and some produce attractive fruits which last until winter. Sun loving, though
also succeeding in shade, they prefer well-drained soil and in this situation even the
more tender forms are likely to prove more hardy.*

*Pruning is best done at least every year and stems can either be cut to the ground to
produce young vigorous growth or to about half the height of the shrub.*

H. androsaenum is one of the best species for shade, abundant small yellow flowers
in June with prominent anthers, and in late summer red and then black fruits. 75 cm.
Of similar habit and size but preferring sun are **H. indorum** 'Hysan' and **H. 'Gold
Penny'**, both very hardy and with red and black fruits until winter frosts. **H. 'Hidcote'**
is deservedly popular for its superb summer-long show of golden-yellow cup-shaped
flowers. 200 cm. Considered a menace in many gardens **H. calycinum** has its uses as
ground cover in the most inhospitable places, shade and dry banks but is invasive.
Golden-yellow flowers in midsummer. 30 cm. Distinctive are **H. prolificum** to 60 cm,
with narrow leaves and myriads of large bright yellow flowers from July to October and
H. 'Ysella', with bright golden-yellow leaves, a superb contrast to other shrubs, but
not to the yellow flowers. 45 cm.

Ilex

*The Hollies contain a vast range of species and varieties many of which grow into quite
large trees, and most but not all are evergreen.*

Hollies will grow well on most soils in sun or shade though they will be slow to establish in drier shady positions. *Best to purchase container plants which can be planted at any time of year if watering needs are attended to.*

Pruning or trimming will, of course, be necessary for hedges but may be also advisable if you wish to retain shrub rather than tree-like proportions on some of your specimens. Other operations are best done in spring, but tidying up can also take place in summer.

There are so many species and varieties to choose from that, armed with the above information I shall have to suggest you look in garden centres or in specialist catalogues for a selection to suit your tastes.

The most commonly known is **Ilex aquifolium**, the English Holly, but as with most Hollies it is only the female which has berries and to produce these successfully it will need a male near by for pollination. There are a few self-fertile varieties such as **I. a. 'J. C. van Tol'** and **I. a. 'Pyramidalis'** which produce berries freely without assistance. The former is excellent for hedging. There are also dwarf types, mostly in the Japanese Hollies, **I. crenata**, bushy and quite unlike the well-known English Holly, and a deciduous species, **I. verticillata**, which has red fruits but needs both sexes to produce them.

Indigofera

A little-known group of shrubs related to the pea family which, though late starting into growth, flower almost continuously through summer and into autumn. These are mostly pink through to purple on leafy stems from 30 to 200 cm. They prefer sunny well-drained soils and, although frost may completely kill above-ground foliage, they will produce new growth in May from below. Pruning consists of tidying up or cutting back older wood to the required height in April.

The most offered form is **I. gerardiana**, growing to about 120–150 cm, with leafy stems producing delicate sprays of rose-pink flowers. Look for the dwarfer **I. decora** which grows to 60 cm, a choice plant with long deep, rose-pink drooping racemes of flowers, or the equally attractive **I. d. 'Alba'** with white flowers. These flower from June to September.

Indigofera decora

Jasminum nudiflorum

Kalmia 'Ostbo Red'

Kerria japonica 'Pleniflora'

Jasminum

Though there are other species one can hardly write on shrubs without mentioning the Winter Jasmine, J. nudiflorum, which though most often grown as a climber makes an excellent spreading shrub, or can be trained to mound over a stump or post, where its long slender branches can cascade downwards. Free flowering and fragrant, the golden-yellow flowers make a brave display often from November until March. Site on free-draining soil with any but an easterly aspect. Whether on walls or as a free-standing shrub, pruning back long shoots after flowering will be beneficial.

Kalmia

These are among the most beautiful of evergreen shrubs, resembling Rhododendrons and, like them, requiring acid soils with the addition of leaf-mould or peat, full sun or light shade where not too dry.

K. angustifolia 'Rubra', growing to 60 cm, has small dense, often drooping, green leaves and clusters of bright rose-red saucer-shaped flowers in June, but the most popular and rewarding species is **K. latifolia**, the North American Mountain Laurel. This is slow growing and slow to flower but rewards with a show of bright pink through to red saucer-shaped flowers in June. Selected varieties have striking red buds and deeper shades of colour, but may well be more expensive if you can find them. Little or no pruning necessary.

Kerria

Deciduous shrubs of some attraction though more often seen in older gardens than modern ones. It is an easily grown suckering shrub with only one species.

K. japonica (150 cm) has green stems through winter, with a fine show of golden-yellow flowers in late spring. The double form **K. j. 'Pleniflora'** is more popular, more vigorous and more striking, reaching as much as 250 cm, with large many-petalled bright yellow flowers which flower in late April and May and often again later in summer. There is also a dwarfer form with creamy-white variegated leaves.

Prune flowering shoots back in June after flowering has finished.

33

Kolkwitzia

Represented by only one species, **K. amabilis**, *this is none the less an attractive and valuable large shrub, known commonly as Beauty Bush. Tall arching branches are festooned with masses of light pink bell-shaped yellow-throated flowers during late May and June. A more definite pink is* **K. a. 'Pink Cloud'**, *but since both will reach 2–3 m by as much across they need siting carefully. Prune if required immediately after flowering to improve compactness, though this may spoil its natural habit, and thin out old and congested wood from the centre of the plant from time to time.*

Laurus

The true Laurels are not the most reliable of shrubs for British gardens on account of their lack of hardiness. In warmer districts where they can be grown they need well-drained soils and protection from cold winds, or, of course, they can be grown as patio or tub plants and brought under protection in winter.

L. nobilis, the Bay Laurel, is grown primarily for the culinary uses of its leaves, though it can make a handsome specimen clipped to a pyramid in a tub or even against a wall. The golden-leaved form **L. n. 'Aurea'** is if anything hardier but best offered a sheltered spot. Golden-yellow leaves in winter and early spring turn a rather dirty yellow in late spring and summer.

Lavandula

Everyone knows the Lavender. It has many uses as a shrub, for low hedging or edging, for foliage in garden and decoration and, of course, its flowers and foliage for perfume. As with most silver or grey plants it prefers a sunny aspect and well-drained soil though it is considerably more adaptable than one might imagine. Excellent for seaside localities. Lavenders require pruning from an early age to prevent stems becoming old and woody and the appearance tall and untidy. Flower heads can be trimmed away in autumn but leave main pruning until spring as new growth is about to begin. Trimming to half the height of the shrub is best if reasonably compact, otherwise more drastic pruning to 5 or 10 cm above the ground may be necessary – but not always 100 per cent successful.

There are many forms of **L. spica**, the Old English Lavender, to choose from, all flowering from July to September, but **'Hidcote'** is perhaps the best, with deep violet-blue flowers borne in great profusion on 60–75 cm spikes. **'Munstead'** is of a similar height and though not so free flowering has larger, more silvery leaves. **L. vera**, or Dutch Lavender, is more robust to 120 cm, with lavender-blue flowers and grey-green leaves, and there are also white forms in **L. 'Alba'** and **L. 'Nana Alba'**, the latter growing to only 30 cm.

Lavatera olbia 'Rosea'

This is a superb shrub for a sunny well-drained location and in such a position will defy most winters, and even if cut to the ground by frost seldom fails to make new shoots by the following May. This vigorous Mallow produces abundant leafy green foliage in early summer followed by a marvellous show of large cup-shaped clear pink flowers, continuing through until autumn. Prune hard in spring just as new growth starts. 200 cm.

Top left: Kolkwitzia amabilis 'Pink Cloud'
Left: Lavandula spica 'Hidcote'
Above: Lavatera olbia 'Rosea'

Leycesteria formosa

All of the shrubs illustrated above, with the exception of the purple-leaved Berberis thunbergii, *are evergreen.* Euonymus fortunei *'Emerald 'n Gold' is a good contrast to the grey leaves of* Senecio greyi *and to the prickly dark green foliage of* Genista hispanica *'Compacta'. Above is* Berberis darwinii *with orange flowers*

Lespedeza

The Bush Clover is related to Indigofera *and similar in respect to requiring a sunny position on well-drained soil to give of its best. There are several species of varying heights but all have pea-like flowers of pink to purple borne freely along the flowering stems in late summer and autumn. Most lose their foliage in winter, the plant dying back beneath the ground but shooting again in late spring and flowering on new season's growth. Clear away any old stems that might remain in late spring.*

L. bicolor makes a medium-sized shrub to 200 cm, with arching branches which bear pendulous sprays of bright purple flowers from July to September. **L. buergeri** is more spreading in habit to 75 cm, with purple and white flowers, and the best-known species, **L. thunbergii** (**Desmodium penduliflorum**), has large clusters of rose-purple pea-like flowers at the end of 100 cm arching stems.

Leucothoe

A small group of acid-loving evergreen shrubs preferring shade.

The most notable is **L. fontanesiana** '**Rainbow**', a low spreading shrub to 60 cm, with cream, yellow and pink variegated leaves. This and the green, leathery-leaved species have pendulous pitcher-shaped flowers in late spring.

Leycesteria formosa

Worth mentioning because of its usefulness as a tall late flowering shrub of easy cultivation. Known as the Himalayan Honeysuckle, it has erect, hollow stems of bottle-green, and lush tropical-looking pointed green leaves. Funnel-shaped flowers are white and surrounded by attractive claret-coloured bracts. Best on good soils in sun or part shade. Prune hard back in March or April at least every other year. 200 cm.

Ligustrum

Perhaps the Privets are the most widely seen hedges in suburban Britain and became so because of a deserved reputation for adaptability to a wide range of soils and situations. They are less well thought of these days because of their apparent dullness and for the fact that they need constant clipping to look their best.

L. vulgare, the Common Privet, **L. japonicum**, the Japanese Privet, and **L. ovalifolium** are the most used for hedges, with the latter small oval-leaved species the favourite. All are evergreen except in extreme winters when leaves will drop after severe frost. These and other species produce white flowers in midsummer, considered sweetly fragrant at one end of the scale to distastefully pungent at the other!

There are more colourful forms which can be used for hedging or as individual shrubs, **L. ovalifolium** '**Argenteum**', silver leaved, or the bright yellow **L. o.** '**Aureum**'. **L. vulgare** '**Aureum**' has larger golden-yellow leaves. The larger growing **L. lucidum** will attain tree-like proportions if left untrimmed and it has two coloured forms in **L. l.** '**Tricolor**' and **L. l.** '**Excelsum Superbum**', the latter with leaves mottled and margined yellow and cream. Those that are allowed to flower freely as shrubs often produce black berries in autumn.

Ligustrum vulgare *'Aureum' with the purple-leaved* Prunus cistena

Lonicera nitida *'Baggesens' Gold', against the contrasting* Sedum spectabile

Lonicera

Though most people will immediately associate the Honeysuckles as the fragrant-flowered climbing plants, there are many worthwhile species belonging firmly in the traditional shrub form.

Such species include **L. nitida**, a small-leaved evergreen used extensively as a hedging plant, and its golden-leaved variety **L. n. 'Baggesens' Gold'**. If either of these plants is used for a hedge it should be kept below 100 cm, otherwise some support will be needed. They will also require constant clipping. A useful but not particularly attractive shrub used for ground cover is **L. pileata**, planted because it will grow in the shade of trees and on banks. Though there are many other worthwhile shrubby Loniceras, I should at least mention **L. fragrantissima** because its small scented yellow flowers appear in the middle of winter. Few are fussy as to soils, most will take, and indeed may require, pruning. Prune flowering types immediately flowers have finished and hedging plants by at least a third when planting and then in May and late summer to the required width and height.

Magnolia

Few plants excite the imagination as do the Magnolias with their exotic tulip-like flowers in spring. There is a vast range of species and varieties, many of which are barely hardy in much of the British Isles and many more which eventually develop into quite sizeable trees. They are not particularly difficult as to soil requirements though they prefer good humus-rich soils where moisture is available. Most are deciduous, flowering in spring before leaves appear. They generally adapt well to city or town conditions. Pruning will probably only be required to prevent plants getting too big and this can be done by carefully thinning or pruning back branches immediately after flowering.

For the smaller garden I recommend **M. stellata** and its varieties, of broad spreading habit but seldom exceeding 300 cm, and covered by masses of many-petalled flowers in spring. **M. stellata** is pure white, **M. s. 'Rosea'**, flushed pink and **M. s. 'Rubra'** deep pink, while **M. s. 'Waterlily'** has larger creamy-white semi-double flowers.

Magnolia stellata

M. liliflora × stellata *'Jane'*

M. liliflora makes a rather larger shrub, flowering in late April and continuing into June with goblet-shaped flowers, purple on the outside and creamy white inside, continuing while new leaves appear. Some crosses between the species *M. liliflora* and *M. stellata* have produced some other excellent dwarfer varieties for the smaller garden – look for these with names like 'Betty', 'Jane' and 'Susan'.

The most widely planted Magnolia in Britain is perhaps *M. soulangeana*, with tulip-shaped white, flushed reddish-purple flowers appearing on bare stems. It and its many varieties will get quite large in time. Other easily grown species include *M. kobus, M. proctoriana* and *M. salicifolia*, all good shrubs or small trees with white flowers for planting in gardens where space permits.

Mahonia

Beautiful evergreen shrubs which are indispensable for providing winter and early spring colour and fragrance. They will grow successfully on most soils where reasonable drainage can be provided and best where sheltered somewhat from cold winds. Pruning is seldom required but if a specimen gets untidy or too big it can be cut back in April.

There are several species and varieties of Mahonia, all with quite glossy, somewhat leathery leaves. *M. aquifolium*, the Oregon Grape, is one of the dwarfest to 100 cm, and adaptable to sun or quite dense shade. Clusters of flowers appear in spring on the end of the shoots, followed by blue-black fruits. A purple-leaved form, *M. a.* 'Atropurpurea', is taller and more decorative but for garden value *M. a.* 'Apollo' must take some beating with its larger leaves and large heads of rich golden-yellow flowers in March and April. 120 cm.

The earliest flowering Mahonias are in the **media** group of hybrids, crosses between *M. lomariifolia* and *M. japonica*. With long, pointed and spiny leaves and long racemes of scented yellow flowers these start into flower sometimes as early as November, lasting through until January or February, depending upon their position and the severities of the climate. Both *M.* × *m.* 'Winter Sun' or *M.* × *m.* 'Charity' can be recommended. Perhaps best of all is *M. japonica*, a large shrub with drooping golden-yellow flowers providing fragrance in late winter and lasting many weeks.

Mahonia aquifolium *'Apollo'*   M. × m. *'Winter Sun'*

Neillia affinis

P. suffruticosa 'Sitifukujin'

Neillia

Little-known deciduous shrubs related to the Spiraea family but worth considering for their attractive foliage, long flowering period and ease of culture. Green, toothed leaves and small pink clusters of flowers at the end of the growing tips.

Look for **N. thibetica**, reaching 200 cm, or the slightly dwarfer **N. affinis**, both flowering in May and June and sometimes later. Prune if required after flowering by shortening branches or thin out congested stems on older plants.

Olearia

This family of sun-loving evergreens commonly known as Daisy Bushes are worth mentioning because of their daisy-like flowers, though few are reliably hardy except in southern and westerly parts of the British Isles. Ideal for sunny spots on well-drained soils and at home in warmer seaside climates, withstanding exposure well. Flowers, usually in mid to late summer, are mostly in degrees of white.

Osmanthus

A small family of evergreen shrubs somewhat similar to the Hollies.

O. delavayi, with its dark green oval leaves and masses of small, tubular fragrant flowers in late spring, is a notable shrub, growing in sun or part shade to 200 cm. **O. heterophyllus (syn. O. ilicifolius)** with its dark green holly-like leaves can be used as a hedge, but better forms for garden shrubs are **O. h. 'Aureus'** with golden-yellow leaves, **O. h. 'Purpureus'**, greenish purple, and **O. h. 'Variegatus'** with leaves edged creamy white. These varieties will be best in a sunny, well-drained position protected from cold easterly winds.

Paeonia

The so-called Tree Paeonias are in reality slow growing shrubs seldom exceeding 200 cm.

There are some species with attractive foliage such as **P. delavayi** with crimson flowers, **P. lutea**, or the improved **P. l. ludlowii** with large golden-yellow flowers, but for sheer spectacle it would be difficult to beat the varieties of Moutan Paeony, *P. suffruticosa*. These originated in China and both Chinese and Japanese forms have been bred over many centuries to produce a wide range of flowers, 15 cm or more across and in many colours. These are mostly double and semi-double, appearing in May. The Moutans are adaptable to both alkaline and acid soils where reasonable drainage exists and, although growing successfully in sun or part shade, are best protected against spring frosts. It is essential to plant them in well-prepared soil with added humus with the grafted union 6–10 cm below the soil level. Little pruning will be required except to remove such dead stems or leaves as occur.

Pernettya mucronata

Evergreen acid-loving shrubs with erect spiky foliage, and although they do have masses of small flowers in summer, they are mostly grown for their extremely bright and showy marble-like fruits occurring in white, crimson, pink and coral. For free fruiting they will be best planted in groups containing a male for fertilisation in sun or part shade. Many named varieties are available. Prune long extended growths back in summer to display berries.

Perovskia

Useful sun-loving grey-leaved deciduous shrubs with aromatic foliage. There are two or three species, all rather similar but equally attractive with 100 cm spikes of lavender-blue in late summer

Look for *P. atriplicifolia* 'Blue Spire' which is particularly good. They will grow happily in any well-drained soil. Prune back at least every other year to 50 cm or so in March or April.

Philadelphus

The deservedly popular Mock Oranges are so called because of their fragrant flowers reminiscent of orange blossom. There is a very wide range of species and varieties, growing from 100 cm to 300 cm, nearly all with white flowers and as garden shrubs generally easy to please and very hardy. Best in sun with good drainage. Pruning should be carried out immediately after flowering has finished in late June or July, shortening flowering stems to where new shoots are showing.

P. atriplicifolia *'Blue Spire'*   Philadelphus *'Manteau d'Hermine'*

Try *P.* **'Belle Etoile'**, which has white fragrant flowers with a central splash of maroon and growing to 250 cm, *P.* **'Beauclerk'**, smaller at 200 cm, with large single flowers stained cerise, and *P.* **'Bouquet Blanc'**, quite different with clusters of double sweetly scented white flowers and quite compact. Dwarfest of all to 100 cm is *P.* **'Manteau d'Hermine'** with double creamy-white scented flowers. Colourful foliage can be obtained in *P. coronarius* **'Aureus'** and *P. c.* **'Variegatus'**, shrubs growing to 150–200 cm, the former with bright golden-yellow leaves in early summer, the latter having creamy white and green variegations.

Photinia

These mostly evergreen shrubs have become more popular in recent years because of their attractive foliage. Medium-growing shrubs, hardy in most parts of the British Isles except in extreme winters, the evergreens are adaptable to most soils where there is sun and reasonable drainage. They can be used for hedging but need fairly constant attention to obtain density.

P. fraseri **'Birmingham'** is a reliable form with large coppery leaves but *P. f.* **'Red Robin'** is more spectacular, making a show of fiery red leaves in spring, summer and autumn. 250 cm. Regular summer pruning will improve density and enhance colour.

Physocarpus

Hardy deciduous shrubs related to Neillia, growing on most soils in sun or part shade.

They are worth mentioning here for an excellent golden-leaved foliage variety, *P. opulifolius* **'Dart's Gold'**. If bare stems are pruned back by half each March this makes a superb mound of broad-lobed leaves to 100 cm, retaining their bright gold all summer.

Photinia fraseri *'Red Robin*   Physocarpus opulifolius *'Dart's Gold'*

Pieris japonica *'Flamingo'*   Pieris forrestii *'Forest Flame'*

Pieris

Evergreen shrubs growing to between 100 and 200 cm, requiring similar conditions to Rhododendrons – lime-free soils and some shelter from spring frosts, preferring sun or part shade. The flowers often form in the autumn, providing an attraction even before finally flowering from February to April with pendulous panicles of often spectacular flowers resembling Lily of the Valley.

For flowers try **P. japonica 'Purity'**, pure white and dwarf in habit, **P. j. 'Flamingo'**, deep crimson, and **P. j. 'Pink Delight'**, soft pink – and there are many more. For foliage there is little to beat **P. forrestii 'Forest Flame'**, which displays brilliant red young shoots in spring, though **P. japonica 'Mountain Fire'** with darker crimson leaves is also excellent. Lastly the much dwarfer **P. j. 'Variegata'**, with small cream-edged leaves the year round, is worth a place in any garden.

Pittosporum

These evergreen shrubs originate in Australasia and, though many are extremely attractive foliage plants, most cannot be considered hardy in many parts of the British Isles. Where a sunny, well-drained and sheltered position can be found some are certainly worth a try to provide additional colour and interest.

43

Potentilla fruticosa *'Red Ace'*　　　　　Potentilla fruticosa *'Princess'*

Potentilla

This range of low growing hardy deciduous shrubs offer tremendous value to the gardener since they provide a good range of colours and a flowering period that stretches from May to November frosts. Not at all fussy as to soils but best with reasonable drainage, full sun or part shade.

There are multitudes of varieties, mostly in the species **P. fruticosa**, with the predominant colour being yellow. Recommended in this colour are **P. f. 'Elizabeth'**, 75 cm, with silvery-green leaves and primrose-yellow flowers, **P. f. 'Goldfinger'**, similar in height with a bushy habit and bright golden-yellow flowers over a long period. Lower growing and good for the front of the shrub border is **P. f. 'Gold Digger'**, to 60 cm, and also bright yellow. **P. f. 'Abbotswood'** is taller at 90 cm, with grey-green leaves and masses of white flowers, and an alternative is **P. f. 'Tilford Cream'**, with larger creamy-white flowers, to only 45 cm. Though other coloured forms will fade during extremes of heat and wet they are well worth space in the garden. Varieties such as **P. f. 'Red Ace'**, 60 cm, at its best a flame-red, **P. f. 'Royal Flush'**, much more compact to 30 cm, deep rose-pink, and **P. f. 'Princess'**, 60 cm, a delicate clear pink. Best colour for these is usually in early summer and again in autumn.

Prunus

Although one normally associates this family with the Cherries, there are several shrubby types of garden value which belong here, some more closely resembling the Laurels.

P. laurocerasus is in fact called the Common Laurel and is valuable as an evergreen hedge with glossy green leaves withstanding clipping well. Of particular garden value is *P. l.* 'Otto Luyken' which makes a sturdy shrub to 120 cm, flowering freely with erectly held white flowers in April and often again in late summer. *P. l.* 'Zabeliana' is lower and more spreading and excellent for ground cover. Another evergreen of value is *P. lusitanica* 'Variegata', a form of the Portuguese Laurel with attractively variegated green and white and occasionally pink leaves. All the above are quite hardy and exceedingly easy to grow given reasonable drainage in sun or shade, though the Common Laurel is not so happy on thin chalk soils.

There are also deciduous shrubs in this family, two excellent foliage species used for hedging, though both will need constant trimming. Use *P. cistena* (see illustration on page 37) for a dwarf hedge with early pink flowers followed by bright coppery-red leaves, and *P. cerasifera* 'Pissardii' or Purple Flash for a taller hedge with dark red leaves turning purple-black. There are many other lesser known flowering shrubs among this family in the Cherries, Almonds and Apricots.

Pyracantha

The Firethorns are indispensable as garden shrubs where they can be adapted for use as hedging or more commonly as climbers against house or garage walls. Evergreen in the British Isles except in the severest of winters, they will grow in almost any garden soil where given reasonable drainage.

Clusters of white flowers in early summer later produce a reliable show of autumn fruits in red, orange and yellow. They are some of the best shrubs for north and east walls but even more effective on those facing south and west. The Firethorns withstand pruning well as wall shrubs, and this is best undertaken at intervals, first in early spring, then to keep back new growths in midsummer and again in autumn.

There are many varieties but if you had room for one only it should be *P.* 'Orange Glow', a superb flowering shrub and reliable fruiting form with masses of white flowers in early summer followed by bunches of glossy orange fruits in autumn lasting into winter. *P. coccinea* 'Lalandei' is a strong growing variety with orange-red berries, *P.* 'Soleil d'Or' or 'Golden Sun', broad spreading with masses of golden fruits, and *P.* 'Mohave' a recent introduction with red berries. There are one or two variegated leaf forms recently introduced which look promising.

Left: Prunus laurocerasus *'Otto Luyken'. Right:* Pyracantha *'Orange Glow' and 'Soleil d'Or'*

Rhododendron

This enormous and popular family of acid-loving shrubs includes the Azaleas and together they deserve a book on their own rather than the brief mention I can give them here. Most are evergreen, with many of the Rhododendrons having large and attractive leaves, but the Azaleas have many deciduous forms. Among the shrubs they have some of the most spectacular flowers of many sizes and colours, with growth habits also varying from miniatures to those of tree-like proportions.

Most of those hardy in the British Isles flower in the March to June period and these flowers can be susceptible to spring frosts, particularly if planted in open or low lying positions. Though they often flower better in full sun it can be advisable to plant them in light shade or positions where they will not catch the morning sun following overnight spring frosts.

Rhododendrons have for long held the reputation that they are only suited to the large garden, but though this may be true of the larger growing types, in recent years a great many dwarfer forms have been bred and introduced, so now there is a tremendous choice of attractive plants ideal for the smaller modern garden. The problem remains, of course, that Rhododendrons will not tolerate lime – but unless you are prepared to go to the trouble of incorporating flowers of sulphur, as outlined on p. 4, you may have to be content with growing them in a raised peat bed or in tubs. Both are options worth considering. Rhododendrons and Azaleas require a reasonably well-drained soil but dislike being too dry in summer, so be prepared to water. An annual mulch with peat, pine needles or leaf-mould will be beneficial in retaining moisture. As a family they make a good fibrous root system and will move easily in autumn or spring, but avoid planting too deeply, preparing planting holes well with moist peat. There is hardly room here to recommend lists of varieties except to say that most reputable garden centres will stock a reasonable range of container or rootballed plants, and much wider selections can be found from specialists.

Brilliantly coloured Knaphill Azaleas: 'Berry Rose' (pink); 'Satan' (red); and 'Golden Sunset'

Rhus typhina *'Laciniata'*   Ribes sanguineum *'Brocklebankii'*

Rhus

The Sumachs are planted mainly for their foliage, attractive leaves which turn glorious colours in autumn. They are easily grown shrubs or small trees for most soils though inclined to produce suckers, and unless controlled can be invasive in the smaller garden.

The two most widely offered forms both have long deeply cut leaves, but where *R. glabra* **'Laciniata'** reaches only 2–3 m, *R. typhina* **'Laciniata'**, the Stag's Horn Sumach, can reach 5 m in favourable conditions. The female form has 12–15 cm 'cones' of reddish flowers in July followed by more spectacular deep red seed pods, while the male sports a smaller green spike. Leaf colours will show best when plants are in full sun, changing in autumn from green through yellow, orange and red. Prune at least every other year to maintain a good shrub-like habit. Branches can be cut to 30 cm from the ground in February, otherwise as a larger shrub or tree prune only to shape the plant. The sap can be an irritant so be careful to avoid touching cut stems with bare skin.

Ribes

The Flowering Currants may be common but they are undoubtedly one of the most valuable of early flowering deciduous shrubs, quite hardy and adaptable to a wide range of soils and sites though best in full sun.

There are several species but those most often offered are forms of *R. sanguineum*, with broad-lobed green leaves of little attraction, though the variety *R. s.* **'Brocklebankii'**, with bright yellow leaves and pink flowers, is an exception. This is an attractive smaller shrub to 100 cm, but may need some shade to prevent leaf scorch. Both *R. s.* **'King Edward VII'** and *R. s.* **'Pulborough Scarlet'** are good, reaching 150–200 cm, with clusters of pendulous deep red and crimson flowers in early spring. An attractive variation is *R. s.* **'Tydermans White'**, with 150 cm spikes carrying white flowers. Prune back shoots immediately after flowering to maintain compactness.

Rosa

The Roses are fully dealt with in a separate book in this series. However, it is worth pointing out that they are in fact classed as shrubs and are ideal to mix in with others listed in this book. I am referring, of course, mainly to the many species and varieties of shrub roses, grown for flower, fragrance and fruits. Much breeding has also taken place in recent years to produce excellent forms for ground cover. Many species can be grown as rambling shrubs, trained up into trees or, of course, used as climbers against house walls or fences. Full details can be found in Book 6, Roses, *written by expert rose-grower Mark Mattock.*

Rosa *'Ballerina' (modern shrub rose)*

Rosmarinus

The Rosemary is an aromatic evergreen shrub known to all, grown best in a sunny spot on well-drained soils, though it is more adaptable than one might imagine. It can be damaged in severe winters, but seldom killed, and makes a useful wall plant or even low hedge as well as an individual in a shrub border.

There are several varieties available though probably the most often seen is the popular **R. officinalis 'Miss Jessop's Upright'**, which makes an erect bush to 120 cm, with narrow green leaves, whitish beneath, and it is these when crushed which provide the herbal fragrance associated with the Rosemary. Long stems carry small light blue flowers along their length during early summer. Trimming is best carried out immediately after flowering.

R. officinalis *'Miss Jessop's Upright'*

Rubus thibetanus *'Silver Fern'*

Rubus

There is quite a wide range of shrubs in this group related to the Rose family. Some can be grown as prostrate ground cover, others, the Ornamental Brambles, have either attractive flowers or striking winter stems. Most will succeed in relatively poor soils.

R. calycinoides and **R. tricolor** are both excellent for ground cover, in sun, shade or dry banks; the former more ground hugging with small green-lobed leaves, the latter more vigorous with large glossy green foliage. For winter stems choose the vigorous **R. cockburnianus**, with prickly stems as high as 3 m but very effective when covered in white 'bloom' in winter. Better for the small garden is **R. thibetanus** **'Silver Fern'**, with attractive silvery-grey fern-like leaves in summer, white stems in winter. Trimmed to the ground each April it will make a dense bush of foliage only 100 cm high. **R. tridel** **'Benenden'** makes a superb background shrub to 3 m, with thornless stems bearing large white saucer-like flowers in May. Prune back to required height after flowering.

Salix

The Willows are a very extensive family ranging from dwarf shrubs to large trees. Most are adaptable to any soil though preferring some moisture, and many are ideally suited to wet badly drained sites where little else will survive. The shrubby types are mostly grown for their foliage, catkins or winter stems, and many that would normally attain tree heights can be trimmed annually or biannually to maintain shrub dimensions.

Into the above category would come **S. alba** **'Chermesina'**, with orange-scarlet stems, and **S. a.** **'Vitellina'**, with golden-yellow winter branches. Dwarfer with black stems is the native **S. nigricans**. For attractive silver leaves try **S. exigua** and **S. alba sericea**. Both will grow large if not pruned regularly but make excellent back of the border shrubs for contrast. For larger shrubs with catkins use **S. caprea**, the Goat Willow, which has yellow catkins, its female form, the Pussy Willow, with white catkins, and for something different **S. melanostachys**, a shrub to 200 cm, with black catkins.

For dwarf shrubs with good foliage and catkins there are few better than **S. lanata**

S. integra *'Albomaculata'*   Salix helvetica

with woolly silver leaves and yellow catkins growing to only 60 cm, though the slightly taller **S. helvetica** with greyish-white catkins and bright silver foliage is also good. **S. integra** **'Albomaculata'** is a novelty with pinkish-white new shoots and green and white mottled leaves in summer. Trim back each in early spring. Lastly, one of the dwarfest of willows, **S. boydii**, which makes a congested shrub of silvery-grey foliage only 30 cm in height and that after many years.

Salvia

Though most of this varied family appear among the annuals and perennials there are several shrub species; few, however, are hardy throughout the British Isles. All are sun loving and require warm, well-drained soils.

The hardiest and most useful group to mention are varieties of the evergreen Common Sage, **S. officinalis** and in particular **S. o. 'Aurea' (syn. Icterina)** with bright green and gold leaves, **S. o. 'Purpurascens'**, purple leaves, and **S. o. 'Tricolor'**, all growing to 30–50 cm, with the latter perhaps the least hardy of the three.

Sambucus

The Elder family contains a range of hardy deciduous shrubs adaptable to a wide variety of soils and conditions. Most are quite vigorous, growing, if pruned in March, as much as 200 cm in one year, with hollow woody stems and leafy deeply lobed foliage.

S. nigra, the Common Elderberry, has fragrant white flat-headed flowers in summer producing clusters of black berries in autumn which can be used for wine-making. There are more ornamental forms with variegated or golden foliage. The golden-leaved **S. n. 'Aurea'** makes a bright show in summer, while **S. n. 'Purpurea'**, with purple-black leaves, creates an excellent contrast. Perhaps most attractive for garden use is **S. racemosa** **'Plumosa Aurea'**, with bright golden-yellow finely cut leaves all summer. Prune all back fairly hard each March for a bright show of fresh foliage.

Santolina

Lavender Cotton. Worthwhile evergreen shrubs for sunny well-drained situations. All are low growing to 60 cm or less and provide attractive foliage the year round with compact rounded yellow flowers in summer. Useful at the front of the shrub border or as a dwarf hedge.

Look for **S. *chamaecyparissus***, better known as **S. *incana***, with bright grey leaves, and its dwarf form, **S. c. 'Nana'**, growing to only 20 cm, with yellow flowers. There are other slightly different grey-leaved species but the bright emerald-green **S. *virens*** deserves wider use as an excellent foliage shrub with button-like yellow flowers making an attractive contrast in late summer. All need pruning hard back every two or three years in March or early April.

Senecio

Though there are several more species in this family there is space only to mention one of the most popular shrubs S. greyi, a first-class grey-leaved evergreen shrub growing to 80 cm and requiring a sunny well-drained position. Leathery oval-shaped leaves are greyish green above, silvery beneath and provide a good contrast to the golden-yellow daisy-like flowers which appear in midsummer. Prune or trim in spring as required to keep plants in shape or more drastically to the ground if severe winters have damaged foliage.

Left: Salvia officinalis *'Purpurascens'*
Below: Sambucus racemosa *'Plumosa Aurea'*
Bottom: Santolina virens

Skimmia

Extremely attractive evergreens resembling dwarf Laurels, seldom growing higher than 100 cm. Most will grow in sun but are happier in shade on moist neutral or acid soils, though S. japonica *will tolerate fertile alkaline conditions. In most species male and female plants exist, having separate types of flowers and needing each other to cross fertilise to produce the attractive fruits. The hermaphrodite* S. reevesiana *is the only species that is capable of producing its own berries without assistance. Because of their slow growth little or no pruning is required.*

S. japonica is the best-known species with leathery, oval-shaped dark green leaves and spikes bearing panicles of fragrant white flowers, the female producing clusters of red berries when a male is planted near by. **S. j. 'Rubella'** and **S. j. 'Bronze Knight'** are male forms with spikes of red flowers attractive throughout the winter. **S. j. 'Fragrans'** is perhaps the sweetest smelling with large white flowers, though the creamy white-flowered **S. laureola** would run it a good second. The self-fertilising **S. reevesiana** is quite dwarf, with white flowers in May and usually abundant red fruits lasting right through the winter, but only on acid soils. There is some confusion within the nursery trade on the naming of these plants so purchase from reliable sources.

Spiraea

A very large genus containing some indispensable, hardy and easily grown deciduous shrubs. Many would be considered too large for the modern garden, but others provide either attractive foliage or flower, often for long periods. Best in sun and tolerant of most soils. Spring-flowering types will need pruning immediately after flowering, the summer-flowering S. japonica *and its varieties are best pruned hard in late winter or early spring.*

S. arguta is a popular bushy shrub growing to 200 cm with somewhat pendulous branches laden with pure white flowers in April and May. Also with white flowers

Skimmia laureola   Spiraea nipponica *'Snowmound'*

Spiraea japonica *'Little Princess'*

Spiraea japonica *'Goldflame'*

but later in June is the vigorous **S.** × ***vanhouttei*** but I prefer **S. nipponica** **'Snowmound'**, 130 cm, with graceful arching branches festooned with white in June.

Dwarfer are the many garden varieties of **S. japonica** such as **S. j. 'Anthony Waterer'**, 75 cm, with flat heads of crimson flowers starting in July and lasting for weeks; **S. j. 'Little Princess'**, 60 cm, dwarfer with pink flowers; and **S. j. 'Shirobana'**, 90 cm, an attractive variation with both pink and white flowers on the same plant. Perhaps the best for garden value are those with coloured leaves such as **S. j. 'Goldflame'**, 75 cm, with orange-red spring foliage turning golden yellow and later green and crimson flowers, and the recently introduced **S. j. 'Golden Princess'**, 60 cm, with bright golden-yellow foliage the summer through, enhanced by deep rose-pink flowers in summer.

Symphoricarpos

These vigorous suckering deciduous shrubs should be treated with care in the smaller garden but they are undeniably useful for their adaptability and for their often spectacular show of marble-like fruits in autumn and winter. Growing in full sun or quite dense shade they generally reach between 150 and 200 cm; some are clump forming and not invasive but others will spread quite rapidly by underground suckers once established. These will need to be removed annually to keep plants in check, otherwise prune plants hard in spring as required.

One of the best white-fruited forms is **S. albus 'White Hedge'**, fairly erect to 200 cm, with insignificant pink flowers in late summer and masses of glistening white fruits in autumn and winter. Lower at 150 cm is a selection of **S. orbiculatus** called **'Magic Berry'** with rose-pink fruits. There are many others of equal merit.

Above: Symphoricarpos albus *'White Hedge'*
Top right: Syringa palibiniana
Right: Syringa vulgaris *'Maud Notcutt'*

Syringa

The Lilacs are a well-known family of deciduous flowering shrubs, many becoming quite large but at their best unsurpassed for creating a magnificent show of flower and fragrance. This particularly applies to the many varieties of S. vulgaris, the Common Lilac, though because of their ultimate size, hungry feeding habits and short flowering period they may not be considered the best shrubs for the smaller garden. The Lilacs are adaptable to a wide range of soils that are reasonably fertile and not too acid. The cultivars of S. vulgaris will benefit from an annual feeding of bone-meal or well-rotted compost. Pruning consists of thinning out weak shoots and congested foliage in April and trimming back flowering stems as soon as they have finished in midsummer. Grafted plants may need to have suckers removed from the base as they appear.

First three popular varieties of **S. vulgaris**, all of which have large panicles of erectly held fragrant double flowers in May and June: **'Charles Joly'**, dark purple red; **'Katherine Havemeyer'**, lavender-purple fading to pink; **'Madame Lemoine'**, introduced many years ago but still popular, with creamy-white buds opening to brilliant white flowers. Of the singles worth considering are **'Firmament'**, sky-blue and very fragrant; **'Esther Staley'**, carmine buds opening to bright pink; **'Souvenir de Louis Spath'**, deep wine-red scented flowers; **'Maud Notcutt'**, pure white with large panicles; and lastly the compact, aptly named **'Primrose'**, with soft yellow-coloured flowers.

    S. 'Bellicent' is one of the Canadian Hybrids, an upright vigorous shrub with fragrant rose-pink panicles in May or June, but for dwarfer varieties try **S.**

microphylla '**Superba**', a bushy Lilac to 200 cm, with spikes of fragrant rosy-pink flowers in May and again in September, or of similar height popular *S. velutina* (syn. *S. palibiniana*), the Korean Lilac, with small leaves and masses of sweetly scented light pink flowers.

Tamarix

Distinctive hardy deciduous shrubs used extensively in coastal districts where they thrive despite wind and salt spray, and preferring sunny well-drained positions where they will grow and flower best. All have very thin branches and narrow plumes of wispy flowers on arching branches. Without pruning they will grow as high as 300 cm by a similar width but annual pruning can restrict growth and maintain compactness.

T. tetrandra is the most vigorous species with light pink flowers clothing naked stems in May. Cut this back immediately after flowering. *T. pentandra*, bright pink, and the deeper rose-pink *T. p.* '**Rubra**' flower in July and August on graceful pendulous branches and these should be pruned in March or April as required.

Vaccinium

A useful genus of acid-loving, mostly evergreen shrubs, ideal for the peat garden, with many species preferring moisture and some shade. Their main attributes are their attractive and often deliciously edible fruits.

Among these are the Blueberries varieties, *V. corymbosum*, used in America and parts of Europe for fruit production. Of more ornamental value are many others, including a delightful form of the Cowberry, *V. vitis-idaea* '**Koralle**', only 15 cm, glossy coral-red fruits in autumn.

Vaccinium vitis-idaea *'Koralle'*

Below: Viburnum bodnantense *'Dawn'*
Bottom: Viburnum opulus *'Compactum'*
Right: Viburnum opulus *'Aureum'*

Viburnum

The Viburnums are a rich and varied family with some superb garden shrubs, both deciduous and evergreen, choice and common among them. Most have white or pinkish flowers, many deliciously fragrant. An added bonus is that flowers often appear in winter or early spring, while at the other end of the year many bear attractive fruits. Most are of easy cultivation.

Of the deciduous types there are many choices; try the winter-flowering *V. farreri* with its erect bushy habit and clusters of pink buds in late autumn and early spring, which open to white sweetly scented flowers in winter. Similar but more vigorous are the hybrids between *V. ferreri* and *V. grandiflorum* offered under the name *V. bodnantense* This hybrid species, and in particular the variety *V. b.* **'Dawn'**, make superb bushes to 250 cm, with large blush-pink fragrant flowers on bare stems from November until midwinter and often later. *V. carlesii* is a deservedly popular shrub for its large rounded heads of pure white scented flowers in April and May. This makes a rounded bush to 200 cm, as does a beautiful selection, *V. c.* **'Diana'**, with red flower buds fading to pink and also sweetly fragrant.

Quite different are the forms of Guelder Rose, *V. opulus*, the species which is quite commonly found in the wild in the British Isles, with white lacecap flowers in June followed by pendulous clusters of translucent red berries. It, like others in this group, has bright green maple-like leaves, with the exception of *V. o.* **'Aureum'**,

200 cm, a first-class shrub with golden-yellow leaves, white flowers and red fruits. *V. o.* **'Compactum'** is much dwarfer, making a broad bush 150 cm high and smothered in bright red fruits in autumn. There is an attractive yellow-fruited form, *V. o.* **'Xanthocarpum'**, which makes a large bush to 250 cm.

V. plicatum tomentosum from Japan, makes a medium-sized shrub of spreading habit with such a mass of white flowers of florets along each branch in May and June that it gives the appearance of being covered in snow, followed by not always abundant fruits. Somewhat similar is the superb *V. p.* **'Mariesii'**, with a more horizontal habit of branching. These both make shrubs 300 cm high by as much across but can be pruned after flowering. Smaller in stature but similar is a selection worth looking for, *V. p.* **'Cascade'**, but perhaps choicest of all is the form from Japan, *V. p.* **'Watanabe'**, which flowers on and off all summer and into autumn. This is much slower growing with a more rounded habit, in ten years reaching 200 cm.

The evergreens are equally useful. *V. davidii* is one of the most popular, with a low spreading habit and glossy green, somewhat corrugated leaves. Noted more for its glossy blue berries in autumn rather than off-white flowers in midsummer, but to fruit male and female plants will need to be planted within close proximity. Taller and more vigorous are *V. rhytidophyllum* and its varieties with attractive green leaves and large heads of white flowers. Excellent background shrubs reaching, unless pruned, 300 cm.

Perhaps the most useful evergreen Viburnums for gardens are *V. tinus* and varieties. These are slow growing, rounded bushes with laurel-like leaves and clusters of mostly white scented flowers from autumn right through until spring, unless caught by severe and prolonged frost. *V. tinus* grows to 200–300 cm by as much across, but it withstands pruning or trimming in April. *V. t.* **'Eve Price'** is more compact with smaller leaves and distinctive for its pink buds before scented white flowers open. Blue-black fruits follow. Equally attractive is *V. t.* **'Gwenllian'**, with rich pink buds, opening to blush-pink then white flowers attractively fragrant. All excellent value garden shrubs.

Viburnum plicatum *'Mariesii'*   Viburnum davidii

Weigela praecox *'Variegata'*

Weigela

Popular and hardy deciduous shrubs with a wider range than many gardeners realise. Not only are there good flowering shrubs seldom growing more than 200 cm, but many have attractively coloured leaves. Generally of easy cultivation in sun or part shade on any reasonable soil. Since they flower on wood produced in the previous year pruning must be done with care. Old wood is best trimmed back or thinned out immediately after flowering, and untidy or elongated stems can be shortened at the same time. Flowers mostly appear in May and June.

W. florida, with its erect habit, has produced two useful foliage forms. **W. f. 'Foliis Purpureis'** has bronze-purple leaves and tubular pink flowers. This reaches only 100 cm and is best used as a contrast plant, possibly to **W. f. 'Variegata'**, more vigorous to 150 cm, with green leaves edged golden yellow all summer and clusters of pink flowers. A rather more delicate textured form is **W. praecox 'Variegata'**, with rather more wavy and brightly variegated leaves, green and white in sun and green and yellow in part shade, so different you might consider them two plants.

For flowering varieties look for **W. 'Bristol Ruby'**, long a favourite with deep red flowers, or **W. 'Eva Rathke'**, crimson. The best white with scented flowers is probably **W. 'Mont Blanc'**, though **W. hybrida 'Candida'** is also good. **W. 'Conquete'**, which has large deep rose-pink flowers, is a worthwhile variety and, of course, there are many more. **W. 'Looymansii Aurea'** may have a difficult name but in part shade it makes a most-attractive shrub with soft golden-yellow leaves all summer. Perhaps most exciting of all is the new **W. 'Evita'**, a breakthrough with a compact habit to 60 cm and masses of tubular flowers in June and again on and off during the summer. It may well herald the introduction of a dwarfer strain to enhance our gardens.

Weigela *'Bristol Ruby'* (above) was introduced by a nurseryman in Bristol, Connecticut, U.S.A., and is a popular plant in many countries. Like all vigorous Wiegelas, *'Bristol Ruby'* is better for trimming occasionally – see notes (left)

List of Shrubs for Special Purposes

This list is intended as a guide as to what type or variety of shrub to select for special sites or situations. The recommendations can only be general, since local soil or climatic features can very considerably. I suggest, of course, that you always refer back to the detailed cultural comments given in this booklet for further cultural information. Where shrubs are recommended for special soils or situations, it does not, of course, mean that they cannot be used more generally.

SHRUBS FOR ALKALINE SOILS:

Acer negundo
Aucuba
Berberis
Buddleia
Buxus sempervirens
Ceanothus
Cistus
Cornus
Cotoneaster
Deutzia
Euonymus
Forsythia
Fuchsia
Genista
Hebe
Hibiscus syriacus
Hypericum
Ilex
Kerria
Kolkwitzia
Lavandula
Laurus nobilis
Ligustrum
Lonicera
Olearia
Philadelphus
Photinia
Physocarpus
Potentilla fruticosa
Prunus lusitanica
Pyracantha
Rhus (majority)
Ribes
Rosa (majority)
Rosmarinus
Sambucus
Santolina
Senecio
Spiraea
Symphoricarpos
Syringa
Weigela

SHRUBS FOR ACID SOILS:

There are a great many shrubs which while not termed 'acid loving' will grow quite successfully in acid soils but this list is of those shrubs requiring acid soils (or a pH below 6·5) to thrive. See notes on page 4.

Andromeda
Calluna
Camellia
Enkianthus
Erica – summer flowering types
Fothergilla
Gaultheria

Kalmia
Leucothoe
Pernettya
Pieris
Rhododendron (and Azalea)
Vaccinium

SHRUBS FOR SEASIDE GARDENS:
Choisya ternata
Cotoneaster (several varieties)
Cytisus (several varieties)
Elaeagnus (majority)
Escallonia (majority)
Euonymus (majority)
Fuchsia (majority)
Garrya elliptica
Hebe
Helianthemum
Helichrysum
Hydrangea (majority)
Ilex aquifolium
Lavandula
Lavatera olbia
Lonicera pileata
Olearia (majority)
Pittosporum (majority)
Pyracantha
Rosa (several species)
Rosmarinus
Salix (several)
Santolina
Senecio
Spiraea (several)
Tamarix
Viburnum (several, particularly
  evergreens)

SHRUBS WITH FRAGRANT FLOWERS:
Abelia (majority)
Buddleia (majority)
Chimonanthus praecox
Choisya ternata
Corylopsis
Cytisus (several)
Daphne (majority)
Deutzia (several)
Elaeagnus (several)
Fothergilla
Hamamelis
Ligustrum
Magnolia (several)
Mahonia (several)
Olearia (several)
Osmanthus
Philadelphus (several)
Rhododendron (several)
Ribes (several)
Rosa (several)

Skimmia (several)
Syringa (majority)
Viburnum (several)

SHRUBS FOR DEEP SHADE:
Aucuba japonica (majority)
Buxus sempervirens (majority)
Cornus canadensis
Cotoneaster (several)
Elaeagnus – evergreen types
Euonymus fortunei (majority)
Gaultheria
Hedera (majority)
Hypericum calycinum
Ilex aquifolium (majority)
Leucothoe
Ligustrum (several)
Lonicera (several)
Mahonia (several)
Osmanthus (several)
Prunus (several)
Rubus (several)
Skimmia
Symphoricarpos
Vaccineim (majority)
Viburnum davidii

SHRUBS WITH GOOD AUTUMN COLOUR:
Acer (several)
Berberis (several, fruits and
  foliage)
Callicarpa (fruits)
Cornus (foliage and some fruits)
Corylopsis (foliage)
Cotinus (foliage)
Cotoneaster (several, fruits and
  foliage)
Enkianthus (foliage)
Euonymus (fruits and foliage)
Fothergilla (foliage)
Hamamelis (foliage)
Hydrangea (foliage, flower bracts)
Hypericum (several, fruits)
Photinia (foliage)
Prunus (foliage on deciduous forms)
Pyracantha (fruits)
Rhododendron (foliage on
  deciduous forms)
Rhus (foliage and fruits)
Rosa (several, fruits and foliage)
Ribes (some, foliage)
Spiraea (some, foliage)
Skimmia (fruits)
Symphoricarpos (fruits)
Vaccinium (fruits)
Viburnum (several, fruits and
  foliage)

Shrubs, trees, conifers and alpines in a glorious profusion of flower and foliage colour. This is a view in early summer of the National Trust for Scotland's garden at Branklyn, near Perth. The fifty-year-old Acer japonicum 'Aureum' on the left remains a shrub for many years, while other shrubs are permanently dwarf in habit

Common Names

Many shrubs have a common or English name, some have more than one and, of course, each country will have its common names too. This is why the Latin or botanical name is used for national and international recognition – difficult though they can be to pronounce. Below are listed some of the English common names with their botanical or Latin equivalents alongside.

Bachelor's Buttons *Kerria pleniflora*
Barberry *Berberis*
Bay Laurel *Laurus*
Beauty Berry *Callicarpa*
Beauty Bush *Kolkwitzia*
Blueberry *Vaccinium corymbosum*
Blue Spiraea *Carypoteris*
Bog Rosemary *Andromeda*
Box *Buxus sempervirens*
Box Rose *Cotoneaster*
Broom *Cystisus, Genista*
Bush Clover *Lespedeza*
Bush Honeysuckle *Diervilla*
Butterfly Bush *Buddleia davidii*
Calico Bush *Kalmia latifolia*
Californian Lilac *Ceanothus*
Checkerberry *Gaultheria procumbens*
Cherry Plum *Prunus cerasifera*
Chinese Witch Hazel *Hamamelis mollis*
Common Laurel *Prunus laurocerasus*
Cornel *Cornus*
Cowberry *Vaccinium vitis-idaea*
Daisy Bush *Olearia*
Dogwood *Cornus*
Elder *Sambucus*
Everlasting Flower *Helichrysum*
Firethorn *Pyracantha*
Flowering Currant *Ribes*
Golden Bells *Forsythia*
Hazel *Corylus*
Heath *Erica*
Heather *Calluna*
Himalayan Honeysuckle *Leycesteria formosa*
Holly *Ilex*
Honeysuckle *Lonicera*
Indigo *Indigofera*
Ivy *Hedera*
Japanese Quince *Chaenomeles*
Japonica *Chaenomeles*
Jasmine *Jasminum*
Jew's Mallow *Kerria*

Lamb-kill *Kalmia angustifolia*
Laurel *Laurus*
Lavender *Lavandula*
Lavender Cotton *Santolina*
Lilac *Syringa*
Ling *Calluna*
Mallow *Lavatera*
Maple *Acer*
Mexican Orange Blossom *Choisya ternata*
Mock Orange *Philadelphus*
Mountain Laurel *Kalmia latifolia*
Oregon Grape *Mahonia aquifolium*
Ornamental Bramble *Rubus*
Pearl Bush *Exochorda*
Portuguese Laurel *Prunus lusitanica*
Privet *Ligustrum*
Rock Rose *Helianthemum*
Rose *Rosa*
Rosemary *Rosmarinus*
Russian Sage *Perovskia*
Sheep Laurel *Kalmia angustifolia*
Silk Tassel Bush *Garrya*
Smoke Tree *Cotinus*
Snowberry *Symphoricarpos*
Spanish Gorse *Genista hispanica*
Spindle Tree *Euonymus*
St John's Wort *Hypericum*
Star Magnolia *Magnolia stellata*
Sumach *Rhus*
Summer Lilac *Buddleia davidii*
Sweet Bay *Laurus*
Tamarisk *Tamarix*
Tree Hollyhock *Hibiscus syriacus*
Tree Paeonia, Paeony *Paeonia*
Willow *Salix*
Wintergreen *Gaultheria procumbens*
Winter Hazel *Corylopsis*
Winter Jazmine *Jasminum nudiflorum*
Wintersweet *Chimonanthus fragrans*
Witch Hazel *Hamamelis*